ANXIETY, DEPRESSION, AND JESUS

Finding Hope in All Things

A A R O N   H O O V E R

WESTBOW
PRESS®
A DIVISION OF THOMAS NELSON
& ZONDERVAN

WestBow Press books may be ordered through booksellers or by contacting:

WestBow Press
A Division of Thomas Nelson & Zondervan
1663 Liberty Drive
Bloomington, IN 47403
www.westbowpress.com
844-714-3454

ISBN: 978-1-6642-9001-3 (sc)
ISBN: 978-1-6642-9002-0 (hc)
ISBN: 978-1-6642-9000-6 (e)

Library of Congress Control Number: 2023901053

Print information available on the last page.

WestBow Press rev. date: 02/03/2023

ENDORSEMENTS

"Aaron Hoover has written an engaging, hopeful book for anyone living with depression, anxiety or suicidal thoughts – especially for Christ-followers who might carry the unnecessary weight of guilt and shame. His honest, vulnerable account of his story as a pastor with mental health challenges dispels the false narrative that pastors don't feel 'that way.' The truth is – many of us do. Aaron shares the practical help he has found along the way, as well as the confident hope that even in our suffering, God is still good and can be trusted."

—Kay Warren, Co-founder Saddleback Church

"Vulnerability and hope is a powerful combination. Aaron writes with an abundance of both. Growing up in a family that struggled with mental health, I nodded as I read. I smiled. I laughed out loud a few times. And I got teary more than a few. This is such a helpful, timely, and hope-filled read! There's a lot of things in life that are over-rated... hope is not one of them."

—Mike Breaux, Teaching Pastor

"This book is an honest dialogue of hope and validation for every Christian struggling with anxiety and depression. The stories and conversation Aaron brings let readers know that authentic faith and community are available and within reach for anyone struggling with mental health. His voice as a pastor whose faith is strong and compassionate meets an essential need on this topic in the Christian community.

—Brenda L. Yoder, Licensed Mental Health Counselor, School Counselor, and Author of Fledge: Launching Your Kids Without Losing Your Mind

"Not only do I wholeheartedly recommend this book, I wish I could somehow wave some magic wand and have it read by the thousands upon thousands of people—suffering in silence—who need to know they are not alone in their fight. I pray this gets to them. I also pray that every leader who serves in the name of Jesus would slow down and pay attention to Aaron's hard-earned wisdom. It could save lives."

—Joseph King Barkley,
Executive Coach, Author, and Keynote Speaker

CONTENTS

FOREWORD

I don't think it will surprise you to hear that mental health has become one of the most significant challenges facing our culture today. If you've picked up this book, it is likely because you are looking for some insight, encouragement, and hope (either for yourself or someone you love). The latest statistics on this crisis are staggering. The sheer number of people grappling with it is heart-breaking. As a pastor, I hear from people struggling with it on almost a daily basis. As a father of teenagers growing up in this current cultural climate, I've walked alongside each of them in their own unique battles with it. Every time I preach a message on anxiety, worry, and mental health, the response from people is overwhelming.

Through all of this, the one thing I've learned is that what seems to bring more comfort and healing for people is not my insights about mental health, or how to overcome the crippling seasons of anxiety when they arise (and they will). What I'm learning is the most powerful thing each of us can do is to *identify* with others in their battle by sharing our own story. This is a crucial part of demystifying the unfortunate stigma that so often accompanies conversations around mental health.

If my memory serves me correctly, I first preached a specific message about anxiety back in 2018. I know, I know—I was a little late to the party. I've learned over 25 years of preaching that the message really doesn't connect with people's hearts until the communicator shares with the audience where he/she has wrestled with the very thing you're talking about. At the time, my most significant struggle with anxiety had been back in 2005, when I was in my twenties. I shared that story in my 2018 message and it helped people. Little would I know my most significant battle with anxiety was yet to come. 2020 was just around the corner.

I realize 2020 was difficult for everyone for a variety of reasons and I was no exception. It was the worst year of my life. June 2020 was the worst *month* of my life, the second week of June was the worst *week* of my life, and Tuesday of that week was the worst *day* of my life. By nature, I'm wired as an achiever and a helper. However, during COVID-19, I felt like I wasn't achieving anything or helping anyone. In fact, it felt the exact opposite! It seemed as if things were falling apart, and everyone was mad at me! No matter what I said (or didn't say), regardless of what decision I made (or didn't make), it seemed that 50% of the people were going to get angry with me...and they did. Many of them sent detailed emails informing me of how they felt and then left our church. It was painful. During the second week of June, things had reached a fever pitch within our country, our culture, and our church. As I was doing my best to pastor others through the crisis, my mental health unraveled. That Tuesday morning, as I was preparing to write a challenging message from God's Word that spoke directly to what we were seeing within the culture, my mom called to inform me my grandmother had passed away rather unexpectedly. The family wanted me to preach at her funeral later that week, which meant I would need to finish writing a message filled with all sorts of cultural landmines *by the end of the day and record it in front of a camera the next day* so it could be shown on the weekend while I was out of town!

I lost it.

It was the closest I'd ever come to resigning from a job I absolutely love and a church I adore. I didn't want to do it anymore. I couldn't think of any legitimate reason why I should. I could feel the anxiety in my body as my thoughts "ruminated" on worst-case scenarios. I spent the rest of the day writing and weeping (and praying for God to release me). Finally, with the encouragement of my wife, I called a friend and asked him to come over. I told him I didn't need him to fix anything, provide any answers, or to even cheer me up. *I just needed him to sit with me.* And he did. We sat on my front porch and cried together. That was the beginning of healing and hope for me.

What I love about the book you've got in your hands is that Aaron Hoover provides this sort of listening ear, ironically, as you read his written words. Working with Aaron over the past several years, I've had hours of observing how thoughtful and wise he can be in the midst of challenging circumstances. I've witnessed the compassion he has for every person he crosses paths with. I've observed how he's navigated his own bouts with anxiety and mental health. Therefore, I knew his book would be filled with insights spilling out of his real life experience with the subject. However, what he's written has exceeded all my expectations. The combination of empathy, theology, and practical counsel found on these pages is rare. Aaron's pastoral heart bleeds through as he talks about something we've all struggled with or faced (in our own lives or the people we love) but aren't always sure what to say. He sheds light on something often shrouded in darkness. I can't recommend it highly enough. Let his words sit with you to comfort, convict, and challenge the way you think about mental health—yours and those you care about.

Aaron Brockett
Lead Pastor, Traders Point Christian Church

To my wife and best friend, Megan. Thank you for walking with me through the darkest moments of life. I pray these pages honor you as much as you deserve and give you a glimpse into the difference you've made. I wouldn't be here and none of this would happen without you.

To my boys, Wesley, Abram, and Roman. Thank you for your unconditional love for me. You are why I keep pressing on. I pray these pages give you courage and that you know unequivocally how strong your mama is and how good Jesus is. Go change the world.

CHAPTER ONE

THE PROBLEM OF RIGHT NOW

"I would've taken my life by now if I didn't have a dog to take care of. Even though I'm not a Christian, I know you're a pastor, and I thought, if anyone would know what to say to me right now, it might be you."

When I saw my uncle Dennis was calling, I almost didn't answer out of fear I would wake up our newborn. My wife and I were sleep-deprived, and I was taking the first shift that night, holding my son's pacifier and watching *Seinfeld* on minimal volume. Since I had moved away from my hometown fifteen years prior, my uncle and I didn't talk very often because of the distance. So his call surprised me.

I'm so glad I answered. He immediately began to share with me he was under the weight of severe anxiety and depression. He had been suffering for a long time. He lived with chronic pain after a terrible accident at work a few decades earlier, which nearly paralyzed him. He had one very close friend, but outside of that, he was isolated and alone.

Through tears, he described his agony and then gave me the opportunity to respond.

After several years as a pastor, I can confidently say this type of interaction *is a thing*. At the most unexpected times, people will look to me as if I have access to a lifeline to heaven they don't have.

I sat for several seconds in the weight of that moment, and the only thing I could think to say was simply, "Uncle Dennis, me too."

I was only six weeks removed from the lowest season in my life, where I also felt the unrelenting weight of anxiety and depression. I'll share more of my story later, but suffice it to say I was every bit the same as my uncle in that season. But he had no idea. The reality is not many people around me knew. And nobody around him knew about his suffering until he called me that night.

Unfortunately, my uncle's experience is common. Millions of people—followers of Jesus and non-followers, churched and unchurched—are suffering in their mental health right now, and nobody around them knows. They feel alone in their struggle. They feel like nobody sees them. They feel like they've done something wrong. Some may feel like they're running out of options. A small percentage may muster up the courage to call someone and ask for help. And an even smaller percentage are receiving what they need when they finally reach out.

I feel compelled to write this book because I believe there is a significant gap in the conversation on mental health in the church. Most books, from Christians and non-Christians, on the topic tend to oversimplify the issue by painting a picture of how to overcome anxiety and depression in a few easy steps. Currently, the ten best-selling books about anxiety have these words in their titles: *End, Overcome, Conquer, Eliminate, Silence, Declutter, Change, Get Over, Take Control, and Calm Down.*

Yes, you're reading that list correctly. I've read it dozens of times and am still surprised the current approach is *overwhelmingly* to simply stop it. Cue Bob Newhart on *Mad TV* yelling, "Stop it! We don't go there. Don't do that. Just stop it!"

On the one hand, I understand why these books are written and why they're read. I've often bought self-help books hoping to find a nugget or two that could give me the peace I sought. On the other hand, I've naïvely thought at times, if I applied a book's teachings, my anxiety would be eliminated. I always closed the back cover discouraged because it didn't do that. And that's been a massive realization for me on this journey.

The idea that we can simply apply an overnight solution to eradicate anxiety, depression, or more generally, any of our struggles, no matter what they are, is not super helpful, and I would go as far as to say it's not even biblical. Instead, the Bible teaches us our suffering and faith often coexist. We don't just need hope that our suffering will go away. We need hope that even in the midst of suffering, *God is still good.*

My current job description emphasizes the need to solve problems that come up. And anyone who solves problems regularly as part of their job will tell you, to have success, you must first identify the problem.

I want to be clear about the problem I'm hoping to address by the end of this book, and it's not necessarily to help you eliminate your mental health struggle. If you're looking for that in a book, check out the ten best-sellers above. When you finish this book, I want you to know, first and foremost, YOU ARE NOT ALONE. Despite the variations in each of our stories, there's not a scenario in the world where you are alone in your struggle with mental health issues.

Also, I want you to know you are not less than. You may feel like it at times—I certainly have. But fighting this battle doesn't mean you have done anything wrong or that you simply can't comprehend what other people easily can. You are in a legitimate war, and I want to honor your courage. As a pastor, I want you to know I too have struggled and can identify with you in many ways.

Last, I want you to know there's a God who is with you. Maybe you've heard otherwise. Perhaps you expect he's upset with you or he's disappointed in your struggle. The truth is there is a God who promises never to leave you, and he's sovereign over every minute of your pain and difficulty. He sees you, he loves you, and he will sustain you.

The story of Zechariah and Elizabeth is a powerful example of the relationship between suffering and faith. According to Luke 1, this couple longed for a child. However, it was God's plan to have them wait despite being righteous and blameless in all the commandments. Think about that—it wasn't their lack of goodness that delayed the answer to their prayer for a child, but God allowed pain and difficulty because he had a line of sight to how it would be used.

Their sin didn't cause their struggle. It wasn't because they weren't praying enough. As hard as it would've been to comprehend in the moment, they were without children because God knew the timing that was best. Elizabeth eventually gave birth to John the Baptist, who played a critical role in pointing people toward Jesus. When an angel appeared to Zechariah to share news of the upcoming birth, he said, "Your prayer has been heard" (Luke 1:13 NIV).

How many thousands of times do you think they prayed for a child? They were faithful for so long, yet they were hurting.

So many people are hurting right now. The church has an excellent opportunity to meet hurting people exactly where they are and to point them toward Jesus. However, that's not happening in so many instances—too many instances.

Instead, the church is adding shame and punishment to the growing list of pains weighing people down. Why is that happening? What can we do to change that? I believe change begins with a conversation. That's what I'm aiming to do through this book. I want to start a dialogue where we can be honest about the complicated relationship between mental health and the church, look at what the Bible says about it, and find life-giving peace in our pain.

I pray, through the words on these pages, you feel seen and loved *just as you are.*

Ask Yourself

- Would you say you struggle with anxiety, depression, or another mental illness?
- If yes, do you feel like you can talk openly with someone about it?
- Write down the names of one to three people you can talk to if you ever need to.

CHAPTER TWO

JESUS ISN'T THE PROBLEM

Mental pain is less dramatic than physical pain, but it is more common and also more hard to bear. The frequent attempt to conceal mental pain increases the burden: it is easier to say "My tooth is aching" than to say "My heart is broken."

—C. S. Lewis

When I was a child, my family attended a church with the word "faith" in its name. What initially began as a body of believers focused on the biblical tenets of a church seen in Acts 2 (teaching, worship, community, and outreach) eventually became a cult focused primarily on faith healing. What was once appropriate teaching of "have faith in God" ultimately transitioned to "have faith in faith."

People in the church didn't visit doctors under any circumstance, and medicine was the last resort, if it was used at all. If you had enough faith, you would be healed. The equation was simple, albeit reckless and irresponsible. The consequences were fatal. Knowing the atrocities my older siblings and hundreds of others witnessed and endured is incredibly heartbreaking.

Many of us would agree this church's stance on physical healing was wrong, and we would be unashamed to say that. However, for those of us who have struggled with mental illness, being told to have enough faith to heal our anxiety and depression happens far too often. The church should be a refuge for people to be candid about their battle for mental health. Actually, the church should be a refuge for people to be honest about anything, right? So why isn't it?

Maybe we've lost sight of what the Bible says about struggle, faithfulness, and empathy. Perhaps we've forgotten the passages in Galatians, Ephesians, and Colossians, where we are given the command to "bear one another's burdens." The Greek for "bear" means to "endure, have patience with, suffer, and persist." I can count on one hand the number of people from within the church who have endured mental illness *with* me, the people who have suffered *alongside* me. Unfortunately, you might say the same thing. And that must change.

A well-known church leader wrote a blog post a few years ago about psychology, psychotherapy, and mental health titled "Insufficient Help." In it, he wrote,

> It is reasonable for people to seek medical help for a broken leg, dysfunctional kidney, tooth cavity, or other physical malady. It is also sensible for someone who is alcoholic, drug addicted, learning disabled, traumatized by rape, incest, or severe battering to seek some help in trying to cope with their trauma. There may also be certain types of emotional or mental problems where root causes are identifiably organic, or where medication might be needed to stabilize an otherwise dangerous person. These are relatively rare problems, however, and should not be used as justification for the indiscriminate use of secular psychological techniques

for what are usually spiritual problems. Dealing with the physical and emotional issues of life in such ways is not sanctification! Certain techniques of human psychology can serve to lessen trauma or dependency and modify behavior in Christians or non-Christians equally. But since the secular discipline of psychology is based on godless assumptions and evolutionary foundations, it is capable of helping people only superficially with no contribution toward their spiritual growth ... Though it has become a lucrative business, psychotherapy cannot solve anyone's spiritual problems. At best it can occasionally use human insight to superficially modify behavior. It succeeds or fails for Christians and non-Christians equally because it is only a temporal adjustment—a sort of mental chiropractic. It cannot change the human heart, and even the experts admit that.

Some big assumptions are made throughout the blog—a few of which are seen above. Not that I made a list, but

- Medication is only needed when someone is "dangerous."
- These "spiritual problems" need sanctification, not psychological techniques.
- Psychology can help "only superficially."
- What needs to change in the battle on mental health is "the human heart."

None of this surprised me as I read it because it's similar to what I've heard for a few decades. This pastor isn't alone in his feelings on this topic. And he's not the enemy—far from it. However, these assumptions have plagued the church for so long.

The greatest misfortune in this narrative is it's not based on scripture. Ironically, the subtitle of the website this blog lives on is "Unleashing God's Truth, One Verse at a Time." This two-part blog has over 2,500 words and big feelings throughout—but zero scriptural references. And this has been the norm for a while—Christians speaking so matter-of-factly about mental health without a biblical backing to their claims. That's incredibly dangerous.

So what does the Bible say about mental struggle? Well, quite a lot. In fact, there are so many examples of biblical characters wrestling with fear, worry, anxiety, depression, grief, and life itself that you could write an entire book about it! Wait, that already happened. If you are struggling and need someone to identify with, just open the Bible. If you know someone who is struggling and you don't understand how or why they can't just overcome it, open the Bible.

In Exodus 4, Moses lacked all confidence when told he must go free the Israelites from captivity and repeatedly argued with God over his inadequacy. Eventually, the Lord sent a lifeline in his brother, Aaron, to help shoulder the assignment's weight. In Psalm 6:6 (NLT), David describes deep mental anguish by saying, "I am worn out from sobbing. All night I flood my bed with weeping, drenching it with my tears." Yet the Lord comforts David and continually uses him for his glory.

In Jeremiah 15:10 (NLT), we see one of the most vulnerable accounts in all scripture, where Jeremiah says, "What sorrow is mine, my mother. Oh, that I had died at birth! I am hated everywhere I go." This passage is *significant* in the conversation on mental health. Jeremiah is as depressed as anyone you'll ever meet. He feels the weight of the world. He feels unloved and unworthy. He even goes as far as to say he wishes he had died at birth.

How would today's church respond to Jeremiah's depression? Undoubtedly, it would vary. In my experience, though, the church has quickly dismissed, tried to solve, or shamed in these situations.

> *You don't have to ...*
> *Have you tried ...*
> *You should ...*
> *No, don't ...*

Contrary to the example we've seen at times from the church, the Lord's response to Jeremiah is profound. He doesn't tell Jeremiah to stop it. He doesn't advise Jeremiah to get rid of the sin in his life to be freed from this weight. He doesn't punish Jeremiah or tell him to pray more. Are you ready for this? God *immediately* responds, "I will take care of you, Jeremiah" (Jeremiah 15:11 NLT).

I was thirty-three years old when that verse sunk in for me. I've been in church my entire life and struggled with anxiety for over twenty years. I've had dozens upon dozens of conversations with wise, loving Christian friends and church staff, and I've been given lots of advice on mental health. Yet I've never been pointed to Jeremiah 15:10–11. I've never had anyone listen to my experience with depression and simply say, "There's someone a lot like you in the Bible, and you should see what God says to him."

If that was the only instance in scripture of someone who could identify with me, then maybe we could simply chalk it up to a miss. However, I also wasn't pointed to Psalm 6, Exodus 4, or the many other instances of mental struggle in scripture. Despite my hope that maybe my experience was all one giant coincidence, I don't think it was. I think there's a more significant issue at hand stemming from the church's discomfort to engage with this topic—in honestly wrestling with it.

That's where you and I come in. We can wrestle—embrace the

discomfort, sit with it, seek God in it, and not rush it. The narrative in the church surrounding mental health needs to change, and by wrestling with it more and sitting in some discomfort, I think better days are ahead.

Speaking of discomfort, I've gotten the feedback before that my resting face unintentionally gives people the impression I'm irritated when I'm really not. I promise that's just the way my face is. Well, I want to make sure that's not the case with the words I'm writing to you as well. In case my tone on this topic isn't crystal clear, I think it's essential for you to know I'm not bitter and don't resent any of the churches I've been a part of. I love and believe mightily in the church and God's plan to use us.

My experience with mental health in the church stirs up in me two prominent feelings—and neither of them is anger. First, it makes me sad for the people hurting who are dealing with the shame of their struggles, but it also makes me resolute to make a difference in normalizing mental illness in the church. I've grieved and processed much of what I've been through. I don't have it all figured out, but the Lord has done a very restorative work in my heart through the pain I've experienced. And I know that can be your story too.

Even though I was told many things about my struggle with mental health, the aspects of my experience that make me grieve the most are the things I was never told. For a long time, nobody told me it was okay to not feel okay. Nobody said Jesus loves me the same even if I struggle to maintain my mental health. Nobody told me that victory was coming, that I wasn't alone, or as it says in Jeremiah, that Jesus would take care of me in my pain.

Somewhere today a young girl or boy has built up a ton of courage to tell someone about their pain and struggle despite a lingering fear they might not be taken seriously. What will the response be? I'm motivated to help give that person a better answer than I received.

Though I know my words alone won't fix this issue in the church, I think Jesus can and will. After all, he knows what it means to suffer alongside. He knows what it looks like to have compassion and empathy. He knows what it means to shoulder the burden of others. More than that, he knows our anguish. He knows our pain.

Hebrews 4:14–16 (NLT) says, "So then, since we have a great High Priest who has entered heaven, Jesus the Son of God, let us hold firmly to what we believe. This High Priest of ours understands our weaknesses, for he faced all of the same testings we do, yet he did not sin. So let us come boldly to the throne of our gracious God. There we will receive his mercy, and we will find grace to help us when we need it most."

This passage promises us Jesus will be there when we need him most. Not only is he present, but he also understands. This truth has been a great comfort to me. He knows what we're going through, for he's also endured it. He's sovereign over all of it. He knew it would happen, and he has stayed by our side to see us through it.

Matt Redman captures the heart of Jesus so well in the song "Son of Suffering."

> *Oh, the perfect Son of God*
> *In all his innocence*
> *Here walking in the dirt with you and me*
> *He knows what living is*
> *He's acquainted with our grief*
> *Man of sorrows and Son of suffering*

If you are suffering today, please know you are not alone. Jesus has suffered just as you and I have. Do you know his final words before his death on the cross? *"My God, My God, why have you forsaken me?"* (Matthew 27:46 NIV)

The suffering of Jesus was so brutal and heavy that he cried out to find God in it. Jesus single-handedly wore the weight of everything wrong in this world when he went to the cross. And by doing that, he ensured we wouldn't have to bear anything alone. He's with us. He's with *you*. Let that truth wash over you today.

I was buying a car recently and felt a tension I think exists in the church. When I was looking at, test-driving, and asking questions about the used car, the salesman painted a picture of perfection: excellent gas mileage, great features, super reliable, once-in-a-lifetime type of opportunity to own this beast of a machine. And in this market? Sheesh—this price is unbelievable.

So of course, I bought the thing! I went back to the business office to finalize the deal. As soon as the topic of an extended warranty surfaced, it sounded like I was buying a car with two hundred thousand miles on it, and I'd be lucky to get home without the thing falling apart. The warranty sales guy (I think he had a different title, but let's be honest, this was his job) literally said at one point, "Between my two vehicles, I've had to replace six wheels due to frame damage in the last eighteen months." *Um, have I made a huge mistake?*

I left that office wondering which of the two ends of the spectrum was true. My confidence in the first salesman was lost after talking with the second. Has this been your experience in the church? Maybe you responded to an invitation from a friend to come and meet Jesus. You took them up on the offer because of the hope, comfort, peace, love, grace, and mercy they said Jesus provides. Then as you got closer to the people following Jesus, the more the product seemed to change. *Wait, I can't be honest about my depression with my small group without being treated differently? Can't I ask for prayer for my pain without feeling further shame? What happened to the first product? Can I get my money back?*

I want you to imagine a church where it's genuinely okay not to be okay. Imagine being candid in your interactions without feeling regret as you walk away. Imagine hearing "me too" more than "you should try …" Imagine being able to ask for prayer with an open-ended "I'm anxious" or "I'm depressed," and you're immediately met with great compassion, empathy, and hope.

You may be reading this and cannot imagine any of that. For you, there's too big of a gap between the optimistic vision I just laid out and the reality you've experienced. I get that. I know many people who could identify with you, including myself, in various seasons. But I think you can help make this vision a reality. Even if this topic doesn't resonate directly with you, we all have a great opportunity in these conversations to pave the way for real life-changing progress in the church.

Ask Yourself

- What role do you think faith plays in mental health? Can you identify the influences or sources that have informed your beliefs on this?
- How do you feel about your faith when you experience anxiety/depression? Do you cling to God, or do you feel like he's absent?
- Is there a person in the Bible whose struggle you can identify with?

CHAPTER THREE

THE PROBLEM WITH LONELINESS

Where a people prays, there is the church; and where the church is; there is never loneliness.

—Dietrich Bonhoeffer

I've never really categorized myself as a lonely person. I've been very fortunate to have close friendships throughout my life. I am very much an introvert, so I've wanted to be alone plenty of times. However, whenever I did desire connection, people were always around. Loneliness wasn't something I felt very often.

Mental illness enters the picture, and—BAM!—anxiety and depression made me feel more alone than I ever had. I used to think loneliness only existed in the absence of *people*, but for me, it was even more prominent in the absence of being *known*. In fact, the more people who were around me who couldn't see the real me, the lonelier I felt.

You might be asking, as others have, "But didn't you have a wife and kids you got to see every day?" Yes. "Didn't you have a healthy work environment with proximity to emotionally intelligent people daily?" A hundred percent. "Didn't you have mentors, counselors, and friends

23

you could talk to anytime?" You bet. And yet I felt overwhelmingly and unequivocally alone.

Why? Because there wasn't a single person who could see the fully present me and simply say in return, "Me too." Most often, in response to my emotional vomit, people would try to fix me. They'd recommend sleeping longer, exercising more, and eating better. After long pauses of disbelief, I'd want to respond, "You know I said I'm struggling with paralyzing anxiety, right?"

Or they'd become sad based on what I shared, only adding to the guilt I was feeling. I didn't have anyone who could see me, relate to me, or understand me. And so I felt alone. The great poet of our time, Justin Bieber, describes this feeling so eloquently in his song "Lonely."

> *What if you had it all*
> *But nobody to call?*
> *Maybe then you'd know me*
> *'Cause I've had everything*
> *But no one's listening*
> *And that's just lonely*

I'm one billion times less cool than Bieber, but these lyrics spoke deeply to me when I first heard them, and they continue to resonate. I've sometimes shared my mental health struggle with others, only to be reassured I'm okay because "Aaron, you have it all—a great wife, kids, job, etc." On the surface, it may look like many of us have it all. But just as Bieber says, having everything with no one listening is so incredibly lonely.

Truly being known is an excellent counter to feeling like we're on our own. And for long periods in my life, I didn't feel known whatsoever, and thus, I felt very alone. I have and will continue to extend grace upon grace to everyone who has ever failed to listen to me. I don't hold it against them as I believe we've all mainly been unequipped for these conversations. And I've messed it up too. In the spirit of practicing what I'm preaching, have you ever not handled these conversations well? Yeah, me too. It's okay. We're in this together and will figure out how to do better together.

One area we can improve right now is understanding the relationship between mental illness and loneliness. On the surface, you may know there's a correlation between these two, but I've started to ask why that's the case and if it must continue to be true moving forward. We have a bit of an oxymoron on our hands. Year after year, we're seeing an increase in people who say they're struggling with mental illness. The growth has been staggering at times.

During the COVID-19 pandemic, the World Health Organization reported a 25 percent increase in anxiety and depression worldwide. That was in addition to the nearly eight hundred million people already struggling with it in 2019. I'm not a mathematician, but that means we've likely surpassed one billion people worldwide who are dealing with, at minimum, occasional bouts of mental illness. However, as mental health issues have increased, the feelings of loneliness within the battle have also swelled. We have potentially a billion people struggling, and yet we feel alone in it? I'm praying and hoping we can right that ship.

In a survey published by the Harvard Graduate School of Education, they report that 61 percent of young adults say they feel lonely frequently or almost all the time. Likewise, 63 percent of this same age group suffer significant symptoms of anxiety and depression. That is not a coincidence. Not being intimately known adds to our struggle, and our struggle causes us to think we can't be fully understood. It's a toxic cycle in which way too many of us find ourselves.

When writing this, news broke that singer-songwriter and actress

Naomi Judd died by suicide. Shortly after, her daughter Ashley gave an interview where she shared more details of what her mother was going through. She said, "When we're talking about mental illness, it's very important to be clear and make the distinction between our loved one and the disease. It's very real. It lies, it's savage. My mother, our mother, couldn't hang on until she was inducted into the Country Hall of Fame by her peers. I mean, that is the level of catastrophe of what was going on inside of her … The lie that the disease told her was so convincing … [The lie] that you're not enough, the lie that you're not loved, that you're not worthy. Her brain hurt. It physically hurt."

Naomi was just two days from one of the most significant accomplishments a country artist could ever imagine, being inducted into the Country Music Hall of Fame. Yet she couldn't internalize the positive over the negative. I imagine she really wanted to. In my experience, mental illness has nothing to do with desire or will—it's much more complicated than that.

One of the complications with the conversation on mental health is there is an element of spiritual warfare involved. I believe that is what Ashley is referring to above when she said Naomi's mental illness was lying to her. Now I don't believe that mental illness is strictly spiritual or that it's the result of our spiritual walk, just like physical illness isn't. However, the devil will certainly use our mental illness to try and take us out.

He does the same with physical ailments. For Naomi, this happened through a lie she was continually told, a lie that she wasn't enough, wasn't loved, and wasn't worthy. For many people, including myself, the lie has been that as we are: We're a burden to the people around us. Satan's top priority in this battle is to convince us the people around us are better off without us. We need to call that what it is—a lie; a blatant, destructive lie. Seeing lies from our enemy shouldn't come as a surprise to us. In John 8:44 (NLT), the Bible says about Satan, "He has always hated the truth, because there is no truth in him. When he lies, it is consistent with his character; for he is a liar and the father of lies."

Is anxiety a lie? No. Is your depression a lie? No. Those are very, very real. Do your anxiety and depression make you unlovable and unworthy? Absolutely not. Please hear me if you're being told you're too far gone, unlovable, not enough, or unworthy. It's not true. God isn't the one telling you that. It's the furthest thing from the truth.

The reality is mental illness is relentless. It's not what we choose for ourselves. We'd give anything never to experience it again. And yet it's still here. We can either acknowledge or ignore it.

I'm observing a lot more ignoring than acknowledging, but by rallying around one another and saying what's true about the battle, I think we've got a chance. But we need one another. In Ecclesiastes, we see the encouragement not to isolate, especially when under attack. Ecclesiastes 4:12 (NLT) says, "A person standing alone can be attacked and defeated, but two can stand back-to-back and conquer. Three are even better, for a triple-braided cord is not easily broken."

That matters because we have an enemy who is on the attack. Again, we have to call it what it is. Satan wants us alone, especially if we're struggling.

In 1 Peter 5:8 (NLT), we are told the devil "prowls around like a roaring lion, looking for someone to devour." If we have each other's back, we will have victory. How do we do this? Do we have to literally stand next to each other all day, every day?

Imagine for a second there are one billion people worldwide who have their mental health struggles written on their shirts for everyone to see. If this were true, don't you think it'd be top of mind for us as we went about our day? If I had one of those shirts on and saw people around who were going through the same, I feel it'd be easy to say, "Hey,

I see what you're going through. I'm really sorry. Me too. It's awful. If you need someone to talk to, just let me know."

Those twenty-five words don't fix the issue. The word is still written on the shirt of that person. But visually seeing and hearing they're not alone would undoubtedly help in the epidemic of loneliness we're getting throttled by right now. So start talking about it. Take a chance.

Is it scary? Yes. Is it worth it? Yes. Will you get burned at some point by someone offended that you saw their struggle? Yes. Will it still be worth it? Yes. We have only two options: Go at it alone or try to get alongside someone.

On a few occasions, I've had my mental struggles thrown in my face after being candid with someone close to me. The first time it happened, I withdrew. I was done taking that risk. It hurt. Especially from a close friend, it hurt badly.

But going at it alone was brutal. I 100 percent do not recommend it. The lies grew. The ruminating intensified. The noise in my head became so loud that I was nearing a breaking point. Being on this side of it with more people in my corner, I'd choose to put myself out there one hundred times just to find one person who could relate to me and see me. I'm not going at it alone again.

The church has a great responsibility in this area. If you're a church leader in any capacity, ask yourself these questions: Is our teaching, in any way, isolating men and women who are struggling with mental illness? Are we equipping our prayer teams to provide resources, comfort, and prayer to this critical need? Are our small groups safe environments for someone to share the weight they're shouldering right now? Are kids and youth ministry leaders prepared to navigate this conversation with their students? The church must approach the discomfort and proactively go first to aid others in their attempt to flee from isolation.

Unfortunately, though, I've seen so much of the opposite. I've been in rooms of thousands of people where I felt all alone. I've shared prayer requests that aren't kept confidential, and I've been in Bible study groups where talking about the digestive issues of my aunt's cat would be about as deep as we'd get.

Thankfully, I recognized the trend and knew how unhelpful it was for me. So I started sharing and at times probably oversharing. I told my peers, men's group, and social media followers about my depression. One, ten, fifty comments later of people saying "me too" and I knew I wasn't alone. The depression was still there, but the loneliness was there a lot less.

In some very dark times of isolation, the writing of Dr. Brené Brown really encouraged my vulnerability. In her book *Daring Greatly*, Brown writes, *"Nothing has transformed my life more than realizing that it's a waste of time to evaluate my worthiness by weighing the reaction of the people in the stands. The people who love me and will be there regardless of the outcome are within arm's reach. This realization changed everything."*

Right now, some of you reading this feel like you are at your lowest point. You've tried to get around other people. You've been to a doctor. You're taking medication. You've done all the right things, but you're still desperate for the noise to let up and to find a moment of peace. You're ashamed because you feel like you don't have enough faith, or this wouldn't be an issue.

I've been there. I'll never forget a time when I didn't want to be alone for even one second. I hated taking a shower and trying to fall asleep because those were times when I had nobody talking to me. I was so unbelievably scared.

In the darkest, most alone moments I've ever experienced, the Lord continued to show me there's no possible replacement for the friendship and comfort he can provide us. Unfortunately, I've thought at times people could fill that void. *If my worst moments are alone, maybe I can just always be around people.* No person can fully meet those expectations, regardless of how great that person's love for me is. But God can.

I continue to find so much refuge in his word. Psalm 139:7–10 (NLT) says, "I can never escape from your Spirit! I can never get away from your presence! If I go up to heaven, you are there; if I go down to the grave, you are there. If I ride the wings of the morning, if I dwell by the farthest oceans, even there your hand will guide me, and your strength will support me."

I understand why mental illness is so isolating. I have felt the depths of loneliness personally. And I've seen Psalm 139 play out in my life in ways far beyond what I could ever imagine. When nobody is around to relate or listen to us, the Lord's presence is promised. And that's hard to quantify or explain *until you've felt it.* I'm guessing some people reading this haven't knowingly experienced his presence.

So here's what I want to challenge you with. Believe in it before you see it. And pray boldly he would deliver on the promises in scripture. Just as he said to Joshua, he's saying to you and I right now, "No one will be able to stand against you as long as you live. For I will be with you as I was with Moses. I will not fail you or abandon you" (Joshua 1:5 NLT).

He will never fail us. He will never leave us. He will always be our greatest advocate and our closest friend. Even when we can't fix or eliminate our struggle, especially when nobody else can help us, God *promises* to.

Do you feel alone? You're not. I can say that definitively. A billion of my closest friends and I are with you. You can take a small step today to be known. In my experience, it's the best step you'll ever take.

Please don't move to the next chapter without doing something. Send a text. Make a call. Pray a prayer. You don't have to do this alone. We can change the narrative together.

Ask Yourself

- Can you recall a time when you felt especially lonely? What were the circumstances surrounding that?
- What can you do or who can you talk to if you feel yourself becoming increasingly lonely? Have you ever had someone in your life respond negatively when you trusted them with your mental illness? What happened, and how did you recover?

CHAPTER FOUR

BROKENNESS ISN'T
THE PROBLEM

Yes, we are totally exposed when we are vulnerable. Yes, we are in the torture chamber that we call uncertainty. And yes, we're taking a huge emotional risk when we allow ourselves to be vulnerable. But there's no equation where taking risks, braving uncertainty, and opening ourselves us to emotional exposure equals weakness.

—Dr. Brené Brown, *Daring Greatly*

I won't forget the Tuesday morning in the fall of 2019, when I woke up with several notifications that Jarrid Wilson—a follower of Jesus, husband, father, and pastor—had died by suicide. Jarrid was an advocate for mental health and was very open about the struggle he had with depression. It was heartbreaking on so many levels.

A few hours later, a Christian pastor and author wrote these words to urge the church to stop hiring pastors with mental health struggles: *"Why are churches placing men, who are so candid about their current brokenness, in positions of leadership?"* I wept when I read this, not because I was afraid of losing my job if the church gave into this plea—I have never once had that concern at my church. But I was so frustrated because this debate shouldn't have marred Jarrid's death. He was an incredible man. He made huge strides for the church in the mental health space. And he gave people who were hurting permission to be open about it. I was also incensed by what was implied in this post: (1) mental illness = brokenness, (2) brokenness = disqualification from ministry.

To address the first assumption that mental illness equals brokenness, let's look at the definition of brokenness. Is it a broad term used to refer to anything wrong in the world? If so, then mental health struggles weren't a part of God's original design in creation, and I could get on board with that statement. However, that's unfortunately not how the author's words read. *"Their current brokenness"* doesn't sound like the author is speaking in broad terms everyone would relate to. It sounds like he is suggesting that pastors who are struggling to maintain their mental health have a brokenness that is within their control. It's something personal that they should be able to handle and never share with others. This fuels current stigmas that mental illness is a sin issue, a result of a lack of faith, and something shameful. I strongly disagree with these misguided notions.

The second assumption bothers me even more. Being candid about our brokenness should keep us out of church leadership? Huge aspects of the Christian faith that require some level of brokenness—grace, mercy, peace, comfort, etc.—are only needed for the congregants and not the leaders? Please don't invite me to that church. It takes me back to college philosophy class, where we couldn't keep up with our professor, and he made us keenly aware we were on different playing fields. No thanks. I'd rather sleep in on Sunday mornings.

How in the world did we get to a spot where our brokenness prohibits us from leading in the church? It's not found in scripture. In fact, we see the exact opposite. As mentioned previously, Moses, David, and Jeremiah all struggled immensely with aspects of mental health. Nehemiah wept and mourned for days over the brokenness around him. Job lamented his birth. Martha expressed doubt and anger directly in the face of Jesus. Peter was wrecked by his failure. Paul boasted about his weakness because he knew the Lord was his strength.

I'd go as far as to say brokenness should be a *requirement* for pastoral leadership, not a disqualifier. The Bible seems to affirm this prerequisite—not just for positions of leadership, but also for everyone who follows Jesus.

> *The sacrifice you desire is a broken spirit. You will not reject a broken and repentant heart, O God.*
>
> *—Psalm 51:17 NLT*

> *The Lord is close to the brokenhearted; he rescues those whose spirits are crushed.*
>
> *—Psalm 34:18 NLT*

> *He heals the brokenhearted and bandages their wounds.*
>
> *—Psalm 147:3 NLT*

> *No one is righteous—not even one. No one is truly wise; no one is seeking God. All have turned away; all have become useless. No one does good, not a single one.*
>
> *—Romans 3:10–12 NLT*

Imagine thinking you're not broken and then reading Romans 3. That'd be a tough day. It reminds me, without God, I am *useless*. Understanding and admitting our brokenness is not a burden to our ministry; instead, it's *necessary*. I have found a ton of freedom in this truth, and I've seen it play out practically.

In his book *People Fuel*, Dr. John Townsend discusses twenty-two relational nutrients everyone needs. He splits the nutrients into four quadrants. People need others to be present, convey the good, provide reality, and call to action. Within the need for others to be present, he mentions six specific nutrients every person needs sometimes:

1. Acceptance (connect without judgment)
2. Attunement (respond to what another is experiencing; get "in their well")
3. Validation (convey that person's experience is significant and not to be dismissed)
4. Identification (share your similar story)
5. Containment (allow the other to vent while staying warm without reacting)
6. Comfort (provide support for someone's loss)

In my experience as a pastor, people simply need others to be *present* with them in the struggle 90 percent of the time. That's something I've also learned in marriage. My wife rarely needs me to jump in and fix issues. Can anyone relate? She primarily wants me to listen, and she also needs to hear her feelings are valid.

People seeking support for their mental health are very similar. Instead of responding to "Hey, I'm struggling" with attempts to, as Townsend says, convey the good, provide reality, or call them to action, they mostly need me to be present. You might be wondering what that looks like practically. Here's how I sit with people who simply need someone to be present. For this exercise, let's assume someone has just shared with me their struggle to maintain their mental health.

If I discern they need *acceptance*, I'll say something like, "Thank you so much for sharing all that with me. I want you to know I don't think any less of you for what you're going through. Despite all the pain you're experiencing, I still love and accept you fully—just as you are."

If they need *attunement*, "Thank you for telling me what you're going through. I'm so sorry. I hear you, and that sounds incredibly difficult. I can feel how hard that must be. I'm with you if you ever need someone to shoulder it alongside."

If they need *validation*, "Wow, thank you so much for telling me. I'm so sorry for all you're enduring. If I were in your shoes, I'd probably feel the same way, and I want you to know you're totally valid for feeling that way. You're not defective."

If they need *identification*, "Thank you so much for sharing that with me. I just want you to know I can identify with you. I've been there, and I'm happy to share my experience with you if that would be helpful. And I'm so sorry for all you're going through. I'm here if you need anything."

If they need *containment*, "Wow, thank you for trusting me with that. I'm so sorry for what that has to feel like. I want you to know I'm a safe place if you ever need to get any of this off your chest. I'm happy just to listen. You can tell me anything you want."

And if they need *comfort*, "I'm so sorry to hear that. It must be extremely difficult to walk through what you are. I'm here for you. Please let me know if I can just sit with you and help you shoulder anything. I'll do anything I can to help make it okay."

I've counseled people through each of these dozens of times. Every person is different, and every situation is unique. However, if you're in the battle right now, you may need something off this list. Maybe this book can help, but more realistically, there may be someone in your life who can help meet those relational needs. Don't hesitate to ask them for it. You don't have to do this on your own.

Many people I talk with who are struggling with their mental health have a relational need for identification. It's so helpful to know we're not alone in the struggle. If you need someone to identify with in some way, I'd love to share my story with you.

As is probably the case with most people, there's a three-minute version of my story and a three-hour version. Maybe we can grab dinner sometime, and I can share more with you, but here's an abbreviated version.

I'll begin my story by first telling you about my mom. She has been an incredible woman of faith for several decades, and she's endured the heaviest of tragedies. Her first husband passed away tragically when they had three young kids, my oldest siblings. I cannot imagine the grief and suffering that season brought her, but she grew closer to Jesus in it, and he sustained her. She has stories of being out of food and out of money, and bags of groceries or anonymous checks would show up at her door from people who rallied around her in her greatest need. My mom has always credited the Lord's faithfulness in sustaining her through this time. Jesus met her in her suffering and was with her. He didn't require her to cover, ignore, or move past it. She showed up candidly, broken, and open-handed, and the Lord provided for her every need.

She met and married my dad, and they had three more children together. I am the middle of that trio.

When I was eight years old, I broke my right femur while playing football with my brother. Our doctor and radiologist found what they believed to be a tumor sitting directly on my femur that caused it to break. I remember lying on a doctor's table and watching my mom weep when she heard the news. Despite the fear and grief, she pressed into what God had for us at that moment.

There a few things I remember about that season. Sleeping in my mom's bed, drinking hot chocolate, and doing puzzles with her are a few. But the most vivid memory I have is hearing my mom pray. It stands out to me because she didn't *just* pray—she pleaded with the Lord for him to heal me. And she really believed it could happen. So she kept praying, praying, and praying.

Her prayers were answered over the next several months. What was initially diagnosed as a tumor was deemed a cyst over time and despite staring at surgery and so many other unknowns, I never had a procedure done on my leg.

As I'm sure it would with any kid, this experience significantly marked me. First, in some amazing ways, this is when I first realized God knew me, loved me, cared for me, and that he could and would heal me. I realized he was *real* and that he was more present and more powerful than I could ever imagine. This was also when the Lord gave me a spiritual gift of faith. I got to see firsthand the faith of my mom and the faithfulness of God. It was a powerful testimony.

In hindsight, this is where some roots of my anxiety settled in. Even though the Lord healed me, hearing the word "tumor" at eight was jarring. At that moment, some of the childlike innocence left me, and I realized bad things can happen to anyone.

When I was eleven years old, stress and anxiety hit a new level as my parents divorced. Looking back, this should not have been a surprise. But at the time, I was in complete shock. The idea that my dad would no longer live with us was disorienting. I remember being so angry. I separated myself emotionally from everyone around me. Shortly after, I had my first panic attack, then my second and my third. I had no language for it at the time. The third one sent me to the hospital, but I was discharged and diagnosed as being dehydrated. Nobody was looking for anxiety and depression in a teen. I continued to bottle up as much as I could, and the next several years were filled with rebellion and searching.

Fast forward about twenty years to the fall of 2019, the Lord had gotten a hold of my heart, and he'd given me more than I'd ever deserve in an incredible wife and three amazing boys. I had my dream job in ministry, aligned with the calling he gave me. But I was in an absolute pit with my mental health.

The digging of that pit didn't begin at that time; I believe so much of it started in my childhood. But the enemy exposed it all at the worst time.

I greatly feared failure because I had seen the effects of it growing up in a single-parent home. I put so much pressure on myself to not make any mistakes that would cast a shadow on my wife and boys. I thought very little of myself and not in a humble sort of way, but in a "you could never amount to anything" sort of way. Growing up, I didn't have men in my life who were injecting confidence into me. I questioned if I could be a great dad or if I could be a loving husband.

I was utterly overwhelmed by stress because I didn't have healthy outlets to talk through my feelings with people I thought wanted to and could help. I suffered from an illness anxiety disorder, obsessive-compulsive disorder, and had heavyweight-style bouts with shame and loneliness. I felt at times like I had lost my mind and no one could relate.

In September 2019, I heard a blatant lie from the enemy, bringing me to one of my lowest points in life. It was a Saturday morning, and weekends were often the most difficult for my anxiety. Maybe because I had more free time, less distraction, and my mind would just run a little looser. I slept in and woke up feeling the weight of the world on my shoulders. It was hard to get out of bed.

When I finally did, I heard laughter from my wife and boys in the other room. They were enjoying one another so much. I felt, if I went into the room to be with them, I'd bring the mood down. And that's when I heard it—*you're holding them back.*

I knew it was a lie right when I heard it, but it still was awful to sit with. The enemy pressed in so hard on my fear of failure that he tried to convince me my existence was doing just that for my family—failing them.

Within a week, the news broke that Jarrid Wilson had died by suicide, and the enemy came at me again. *See, you're not alone. You're not the only pastor who is a burden.* Thankfully, the Lord allowed me to see the lie in these comments, and then I saw the post about my brokenness disqualifying me. That could've taken me out, which is so tragic because that's the type of friendly fire we see too often in the church. It's just unnecessary. The enemy tried to use the words of a *pastor* to convince me of something that wasn't true.

See, as much as I want to act like I've got it all together at times, I know I don't. And I've heard the lie hundreds of times inside my head, that my brokenness disqualifies me, but when I heard it from someone else, I could see it for what it is—total BS.

If I have a propensity for illness anxiety disorder, and I'm disqualified because of it, then I don't know how to reconcile so much of the Bible. I'm not stuck in my anxiety, but it is a grind and a battle. And it's a battle through which I choose to run to Jesus. I've never been closer to Jesus than when I'm in a pit of darkness. Struggle, pain, difficulty, anxiety, depression, and suffering can absolutely coexist with our faith. Faith implies tension and uncertainty. It's a weird both/and.

This is why this topic is so important to me. I've lived the struggle. I've felt the pain. And I've seen God be faithful. To me, he's been faithful through his word, through people, and through medicine. He's been sovereign over every minute and every trial. He's allowed it, and he's seen me through it.

Two years ago, the Lord gave me a doctor who recognized my chemical makeup and got me on an antidepressant to boost my serotonin levels. The Lord further equipped people around me to simply sit with me and pray with me rather than trying to fix me. The Lord has given me refuge in his word. He's given me the vision to know many people are going through the same struggle, and he wants to use me in it. That aligns with what I see in Romans 8:28 (NLT), where Paul says, "God causes everything to work together for the good of those who love God and are called according to his purpose for them."

He's called me to use my experience for his good. So here I am, broken, open-handed, and wanting to make a difference.

Ask Yourself

- How can you encourage the people around you in their mental health? Are you seeking opportunities to share struggles and lift others up?
- What are some of the pivotal events in your life that have shaped you and made an impact on your mental health journey?
- Which of the six relational nutrients mentioned in this chapter do you need most right now? Who can you reach out to right now and ask them to provide that for you?

CHAPTER FIVE

THE POWER OF REDEMPTION

Health is set before us as if it were the great thing to be desired above all other things. It is so? I would venture to say that the greatest blessing that God can give to any of us is health, with the exception of sickness. Sickness has frequently been of more use to the saints of God than health has. If some men, that I know of, could only be favoured with a month of rheumatism, it would, by God's grace, mellow them marvelously.

—Charles Spurgeon

Known today as the "Prince of Preachers," Charles Spurgeon burst onto the scene in London in the middle of the nineteenth century with a preaching style that was highly compelling in large part because of his rawness and honesty. Spurgeon dealt with many physical and emotional maladies and yet declared Christ at the center of every moment.

Spurgeon's message was so highly respected that Carl F. H. Henry referred to him as "one of evangelical Christianity's immortals," and

American tourists returning from England were often greeted with two questions: "Did you see the Queen?" and "Did you hear Spurgeon?"[1]

Spurgeon declared the greatest blessing God can give any of us is *sickness*. Come again? What a contrast to the church I referred to earlier, where sickness was a sign of a lack of faith! Spurgeon's claim was extremely bold, and depending on your background, it may even be somewhat offensive. A sign of God's blessing is to be sick? If that were the title of a sermon series today, the room would be relatively empty.

However, what would resonate about Spurgeon today and what drew a crowd then was his lived experience and authenticity from the pulpit. Spurgeon dealt with extreme pain in his life and saw how the Lord used the pain to draw him closer. Spurgeon was faithful *and* was inundated with pain that wasn't lifted when he cried out. I admire his perspective and see it affirmed throughout the entirety of scripture.

> *We can rejoice, too, when we run into problems and trials, for we know that they help us develop endurance. And endurance develops strength of character, and character strengthens our confident hope of salvation. And this hope will not lead to disappointment. For we know how dearly God loves us, because he has given us the Holy Spirit to fill our hearts with his love.*
>
> —Romans 5:3–5 NLT

> *Dear brothers and sisters, when troubles of any kind come your way, consider it an opportunity for great joy. For you know that when your faith is tested, your endurance has a*

---

[1] https://www.spurgeon.org/resource-library/blog-entries/10-spurgeon-quotes-for-wounded-christians/

chance to grow. So let it grow, for when your endurance is
fully developed, you will be perfect and complete, needing
nothing.

—James 1:2–4 NLT

These passages paint a compelling picture of God using our difficulty and pain to draw us closer to him. It's no mystery our greatest proximity to the Lord often happens when we're struggling through circumstances in life. This is clearly one way he uses our pain.

Depending on what you're walking through, this may be extremely difficult to reconcile. The pain is so thick, and the noise in your head is so loud that it seems impossible it's worth what the Lord might be doing through it.

I get that. This is a big reason I can't resonate with the idea that mental illness is an issue of a lack of faith because what I've seen play out in life is it requires *great* faith to keep going amid this struggle. Every hour of every day, I'm putting faith in the Lord that he knows what he's doing and that he has a plan to redeem all this. I don't have a plan for that. I don't understand why mental illness exists. But he gets it, and he's sovereign over it.

I've been greatly encouraged at times in my battle for mental health by finding myself within the characters in the Bible. One person I resonate with a ton is Moses; not because I've led a group of people from exile toward their ultimate destiny, not because I grew up a prince or have had the responsibility of writing God's laws on stone tablets. Despite all the areas I don't relate to him, the one place where I feel Moses and I are brothers from different mothers is in his feelings of inadequacy.

In Exodus 3, we get a front-row seat to an incredible interaction between God and Moses. In case you're not familiar with this passage,

God appears to Moses in a burning bush and ultimately gives him the task of going to Egypt to free the Israelites from slavery. The Creator of the universe, who holds everything in his hands and has orchestrated every aspect of Moses's life to this point, audibly speaks and tells Moses precisely what's required of him. But Moses isn't convinced he can carry out what the Lord has asked of him. The main thing holding him back—he isn't good with his words.

I felt a call into full-time ministry when I was in college. There wasn't an audible interaction with the Lord, but I knew, beyond a shadow of a doubt, he wanted to use me in this way. I was *terrified*. The primary reason was a fear of public speaking I had for as long as I can remember. Just a few months before this calling, I dropped out of a communications class because I had to give a speech. I'm not sure why I didn't know that'd be a requirement when I signed up for the class. But now the Lord was asking me to step into ministry, and I knew that would require speaking in some capacity.

I stepped into that fear, and soon after joining the staff at Traders Point Christian Church, I was given the opportunity for a speaking role at a group leader training. I was brought on staff to shepherd and train group leaders, so this was the perfect opportunity to do just that. But it would require speaking in front of a few hundred of them.

I'll never forget my boss soft-tossing me a question I should've just been able to tee off on, but instead, my mind went blank just a few words into my rehearsed response. I froze up. Looking down at my sheet of notes, I saw what appeared to be a thousand ants crawling around on my paper, and I couldn't muster another word. What I feared so many times had happened, and my confidence was completely shaken.

After that experience, I felt seen in the candid conversation in Exodus 3 between Moses and God. Moses was a man with a speaking impediment, and he didn't think he had what it took. He tries to talk

God out of this calling and continues to repeat, "Who am I?" (Exodus 3:11 NLT) I took so much courage from how the Lord used Moses, who I knew persevered beyond what he thought he was capable of and trusted God to fill in the gaps he had.

I've often wondered what the most significant contribution of Moses was. Was it his role in going to Egypt? Was it parting the Red Sea? Was it leading the Israelites through the wilderness after their escape? Or was it in his weakness and vulnerability that he's made an impact on countless people who have related to him, like me? God has used the brokenness of Moses to give courage to leaders for thousands of years.

Despite my fear of public speaking, the Lord continued to increase my role at Traders Point, and with every new layer of responsibility, more public speaking was required. I wanted no part in any of that, but the story that began with Moses, and I saw continuing with me, was too strong to deny.

In 2017, I transitioned to a campus pastor role, meaning I'd speak in front of more than a thousand people a few times every Sunday. That was literally my worst nightmare. But God continued to redeem my first experience with public speaking, so my trust in him just continued to grow. *Lord, you've been faithful to this point, and I know you will continue to be.*

My anxiety was more present than ever on Saturday evenings, and I couldn't shake it. Even though I had experienced the Lord's faithfulness time and time again, my mind would replay my public speaking failures from the past to the point I'd convince myself it would happen again. I'd rehearse until I finally had to sleep, and every week I'd think back to the interaction on a mountain where Moses thought, *Who am I?* and God reminded him, "Who has made man's mouth?" (Exodus 4:11 ESV)

As I referenced earlier, Romans 8:28 gives us insight into how God uses these types of situations. God causes *all things* to work together for his good. Would the story of Moses be as powerful if he was a brilliant, confident public speaker? Absolutely not. His inability and inadequacy make the result jaw-dropping. And like all of us desire, Moses's legacy continues beyond his years on earth. Even today God continues to provide redemption through the story of Moses by using his example in the lives of others.

God will use our pain for his good. That can be seen in several ways. Maybe it's for our good later down the road to have a better perspective. Perhaps it's for the good of his kingdom at large. In whatever way he chooses to use it, we can trust it will be good. I encourage you to take some time and reflect on how God might want to redeem your story. What have you walked through that others may be going through now or that others will have to navigate eventually?

An example of this playing out in my life is through my marriage. I come from a large extended family and have seen many failed marriages. A question I've asked is, "God, how could you ever use divorce for good?" Divorce is so far from good.

But one way it's been *used* for good is by providing people a picture of what marriage should look like and what it shouldn't. Now I think it'd be irresponsible to conclude God created all the brokenness in my family so myself and others could learn how to have a healthy marriage. I don't believe that for one second. I think it's inconsistent with scripture to believe that God wants anything other than the best for every person, every marriage, and every family.

However, *we are all messed up*. We're sinful, we're prideful, we're selfish. So divorce happens way too often, and that's on us. Romans 8:28 doesn't say God will ensure everything is good. No, it says he will *use* everything for his good. Divorce? He can use it. He's using it in my life to show me the importance of my ministry at home and the fact that my marriage is the most important relationship I could ever have.

I don't think he orchestrated it, but I wholeheartedly believe he's using it and will continue to.

Another example I've seen of redemption in my life is through my journey with mental illness. The Lord is using my experience to make an impact on others.

Would you be open to that possibility? That no matter what you've gone through and how difficult it has been, God might be able to use it for good in some way during your life and after?

Let's say you're ready to allow God to redeem your story, maybe you're wondering what your first step should be.

For me, that began by praying for redemption. I'd love to say this prayer happened at first with a pure heart. *Lord, would you use this for your good, pretty please?* Not quite. It was more out of desperation. *Lord, this is so awful. I can't possibly imagine why it's happening, except that maybe you're going to use it. I beg you to do just that.*

Next, I had to take the step of being more open with others, not with the whole world all at once, but it began with close friends and family, then my men's group, then the people I worked closest with. After a couple of years of trial and error on how to navigate these conversations, that circle kept growing. More people knew who I was, and I got a front-row seat to more of what God was up to.

Also, I would suggest you start documenting how God uses your story. There will be times when you feel like you're not making any difference. The enemy will blitz you with thoughts that your story doesn't matter. *He's lying.* It will matter to so many people—write it down when it happens so you don't forget.

For long seasons mired in pain and trial, I was focused on *my* battle, *my* difficulty, and *my* victory. Opening myself up to the possibility God would one day use and redeem my story got the focus off me. Suddenly, it became about the collective, broader *we* in the story.

Have you ever noticed how many aspects of God's creation emphasize *we* more than *me?* He consistently applies this theme to humans, animals, and nature throughout his creation. Take the coast redwood tree as an example. The world's tallest tree, often surpassing three hundred feet tall, has one of the more shallow root systems, only six to twelve feet deep. However, they will live for thousands of years and grow extremely tall because of an *interconnected* root system.

> Intertwined root systems provide stability to these mighty trees during strong winds and floods—quite literally holding one another down. Their shallow roots can also sprout and support new redwood trees far more successfully than from their cone seeds. Redwoods can often be seen growing in circles, known as "<u>fairy rings</u>" or "<u>family circles</u>," because they sprouted from the roots of a parent tree. The parent tree helps to nourish the sprouts with water and sugars through its well-established root system while they grow. When the parent trees die, the young redwoods continue to grow in the circle shielding, stabilizing, and nourishing each other through their roots. Redwoods will help each other even if they aren't "family." Trees in the ring aren't always genetically identical or clones of the parent tree. Some of the redwoods in a ring can also grow from seedlings. Redwoods take care of one another supporting each other with nutrients through their interconnected roots including their young, sick and old.[2]

---

[2] https://sempervirens.org/learn/redwood-facts/#1

Without the luxury of any communication tools we've been given, coast redwood trees know how to support one another. The older trees understand what the younger ones need to be healthy. I have to think their two thousand years of experience is an asset in this situation. If a less experienced tree came along and the mature ones decided not to connect them into the family and instead ignored their experience, the collective would be worse off.

Your roots, your experience, and your *story* are significant. Don't ignore the opportunity you have to make an impact on other people.

Ask Yourself

- Has there ever been a time in your life with great challenges where you also felt very close to God?
- What is one step you can take toward being open about your mental health?
- Consider praying that God could redeem your story of mental illness instead of simply making it go away.
- Try writing down your story about anxiety and depression. What has shaped you? What has hurt you? What has helped?

CHAPTER SIX

YOUR STORY HAS POWER

The opposite of recognizing that we're feeling something is denying our emotions. The opposite of being curious is disengaging. When we deny our stories and disengage from tough emotions, they don't go away; instead, they own us, they define us. Our job is not to deny the story, but to defy the ending—to rise strong, recognize our story, and rumble with the truth until we get to a place where we think, Yes. This is what happened. This is my truth. And I will choose how this story ends."

—Dr. Brené Brown, *Rising Strong: The Reckoning. The Rumble. The Revolution*

Have you ever spent seven consecutive nights in Downtown Las Vegas? No? Didn't think so. Why would anyone want to do that? Well, maybe you had to for your honeymoon. Allow me to explain.

Megan and I were supposed to be heading to Cozumel, Mexico, right after our wedding. However, a travel warning issued at the last minute threw that into jeopardy, and we began to scramble to find an alternate destination. We had a family member's timeshare membership offered to us, which meant we had two options that late in the game—Branson or Las Vegas. Seven nights in the desert, here we come.

It's possible some people could thrive for an entire week in Vegas. But Megan and I on a budget of a few hundred dollars? Not so much. We went into every single casino and signed up for their VIP membership so we could each get a free $5 play card. Then we made our way to the penny slots and tried to make it go as far as possible while we sipped on free soda.

One night we were buying tickets to a show from a vendor, and it came up we were on our honeymoon. The lady at the kiosk was just getting off work, and she said she had a bunch of coupons in her car she wanted to give us. *We actually walked to her car. Why would we ever do that?* Luckily, she really did have coupons to give us, and we made it back to our room safely that night.

From my experience in Vegas, you can see everything you want and most things you don't want to see in just a few days. I can predict, with almost 100 percent certainty, what you'll see right in front of the Bellagio on a busy Friday or Saturday night—a man "preaching" into a megaphone to the masses about *their* sin and the eternal damnation that awaits *them*.

This type of message makes me cringe. Aspects of it are true, yes. God hates sin. Hell does await people who aren't reconciled to him. However, it's just one part of the gospel message, and it's incomplete. And shouting it at random tourists without the context of a broader conversation and personal relationship, more people are likely to be turned away than are going to be brought any closer.

It also leaves out a critical gospel truth—we have all sinned and have fallen short of God's glory. So for a person following Jesus to point out the sins of many without reflecting on any personal wrestling is so wildly unhelpful to the watching world.

Like many others, I've found myself drifting to be more and more skeptical. When I hear about something great, I usually have some follow-up questions. *I loved that restaurant.* Yeah, what was the bill? *That movie was fantastic.* Run time? *You have to watch this dude hoop.* Have you seen LeBron? I don't just want the good stuff—I want the whole story.

And I'd say that's what we all need, regardless of what we're being sold. If you were to get a snapshot of how I am right now and hear I'm doing great and God is faithful, you wouldn't hear the complete story. I'd have to explain some of the tough stuff to truly show you the beauty of where I'm at today. The gospel is referred to as the *good news*, but the good isn't quite as sweet without the perspective of the *bad*. I believe that's what God's asking me to share with anyone who will listen. It's not "life is perfect" or "life is terrible." It's simply "Here's what the Lord has done for me in my struggle."

I am finding my greatest testimony is one that shares his faithfulness amid difficulty. I'm growing to be very grateful for the story he's given me. Without it, I'm sure I wouldn't be able to connect with the people he's been putting into my life. Right now, anyone can reach out to me and say, "Hey, I'm struggling mentally," and he's given me a voice in that conversation. If I've had an easy life, not sure that exists in reality, my voice sounds very different. My relatability would be lacking, and my opportunities to minister would dramatically shift.

I shared earlier my uncle had reached out at one point to express the weight and attack he was under. My uncle wasn't following Jesus, yet the Lord orchestrated that conversation because of what we had been walking through. After I said "me too" to many of the same struggles my uncle faced, I had the opportunity to say, "Can I tell you about someone who has changed all of this for me?"

He gave me permission to share Jesus with him. He asked many questions and said multiple times "I never knew that" to simple gospel truths. A few months later, he gave his life to the Lord.

I take no credit for that; that was an act of God, seventy years in the making, drawing my uncle closer to him. But I believe he used someone who was struggling and available to say, "Yeah, me too. I know what you're going through. And here's someone who has given me great hope, and I know he will do the same for you."

Your testimony has *great power*. Don't underestimate it. God has given you a story that can minister uniquely to someone today. There are so many struggles I can't identify with, but you may be able to and vice versa. Together I know we can make a difference.

God will use your story. No matter what you've been through or what you're going through right now, I know he wants to use it. My confidence comes from scripture and what I've seen throughout my life. In Mark 5, after Jesus healed a man who was demon-possessed, the man begged to stay alongside him. But Jesus intended to use the miracle in a different way. He said, "No, go home to your family, and tell them everything the Lord has done for you and how merciful he has been" (Mark 5:19 NLT). The man returned to his hometown to tell everyone of God's goodness, and everyone was amazed at what he told them.

In some of the most tragic situations in the mental health battle, stories have prevailed.

Rick and Kay Warren have a story. They founded Saddleback Church in 1980, and it quickly grew to become one of the largest churches in the United States. Their son, Matthew, tragically died by suicide in 2013 after a twenty-year battle with depression. In an interview a few years after Matthew's death, Kay opened up about the stigma of mental illness in the church and how the Lord was using Matthew's story to encourage others who were struggling:

I have so many people come up to me and whisper in my ear, "I live with depression." Nobody should have to whisper about their lives at church. That is the one safe place. I really can't even count in the last 2½ years how many people have come up to me and said Matthew's suicide has caused them to decide not to take their lives. They watched our family and saw the devastation that we've experienced. Some have said to me, "I don't care how bad it gets. I can't do that to my mom and dad, my wife, or my kids." And then there are those that have lost someone to suicide, but our story of resilience and hope has given them the courage to get out of bed.

Nobody should have to whisper about their lives at church. Yes and amen. And if people continue sharing like Rick and Kay have, then whispering about our struggles can be a thing of the past. Matthew's story is tragic. We all wish it wouldn't have happened. And yet God is somehow using it to rescue and redeem others.

Tony and Lauren Dungy have a story as well. They are parents of eleven kids and together have authored *Uncommon Marriage*. Tony is also a retired Super-Bowl-winning NFL coach. In December 2005, their son James died by suicide after battling depression. Over a decade after this tragedy, Tony shared his perspective on what God was doing through it.

I know in my heart James's death has affected many people and benefited many people. I also know that if God had had a conversation with me and told me, "I can help some people see, I can heal some relationships, I can save some people's lives, I can give some people eternal life, but I have to take your son to do it. You make the choice," I would have said, "No, I'm sorry. As great as all that is, I don't want to do that." And that's the awesome thing about God. He had that choice, and he said yes.[3]

I've read that quote so many times. On the one hand, that's an incredible perspective. I'm grateful the Dungy family sees such hope in the midst of tragedy. And I think there's a subtlety in God's hand in all this that I don't want to miss. God will use suicide, but I don't think he's orchestrating it. I believe God, in all his power, can use someone's life just as much as a tragedy, and we have the choice to choose life.

Unfortunately, these stories came at a cost none of us should be paying. These are stories of family members dealing with unimaginable grief because of the toll mental illness has taken on their loved ones. We need to advocate for more stories of survivors grappling with the day-to-day pain but continuing to see God's purpose in it. That's why I'm telling my story, and that's why I'm encouraging you to tell yours.

I understand the hesitation to share. It is definitely easier to keep all this in the dark. At times I've wondered if bringing this conversation into the light is like signing myself up for an attack. Ultimately, yes, it probably is to some extent. But I still believe it's worth it. I want to be part of God using stories to benefit others.

I love the exchange Jesus has with the woman at the well in John 4. If you're unfamiliar with this passage, Jesus interacts with a woman collecting water for her family at a popular well; she also has a lot of baggage and shame. She went to the well at a time of day that would be very unusual, most likely to avoid a crowd because of all the shame she was carrying.

---

[3] https://www.focusonthefamily.com/parenting/tony-dungys-family-surviving-suicide/

As he always does, Jesus cuts right to the heart in this interaction and promises her water that will quench her thirst *forever*. He would take care of the things she was thirsting for and looking for in the world. After this interaction, the Bible says, "The woman left her water jar beside the well and ran back to the village, telling everyone, 'Come and see a man who told me everything I ever did! Could he possibly be the Messiah?' So the people came streaming from the village to see him" (John 4:28–30 NLT).

In one conversation with Jesus, this woman goes from extreme shame and hiding over her sin to blurting out, "Come and see a man who told me everything I ever did!" That's the good *in Jesus* meeting the messy *in us*—all in one beautiful story. The world doesn't need another perfect person right now. Social media is rife with images of perfection. The world needs to know how a perfect God is redeeming imperfect people and calling us to join the mission to get more of his kids back to him.

If you're open to how God might want to speak through your story, begin working on it. Don't just read my story or the stories of others; start crafting your own so he can use it. Ask yourself some of these questions to help you get started:

- What has been my testimony of God's faithfulness?
- When did I first see God moving in my life and in what way(s)?
- What was my upbringing like, and have I been drawn closer to him because of it or despite it?
- If I could make a difference throughout the world, what area would it be in?
- What conversations do I get most excited about?
- What are my passions?
- When I think about all the people struggling, who do I have an extra measure of empathy and compassion toward?

Next, pray for God to use it. Sure, you've heard me say he wants to use it because I've literally never seen an instance where Romans 8:28 doesn't play out just as it reads. He will use it for good—for sure. However, we must be fully dependent on how and when he wants to use it. My story is really God's story that he's using me in. So I need to surrender to his plan in all of it. From the time I first experienced anxiety, depression, and panic attacks, it was about twenty years later when he gave me a voice in this conversation. Now *a lot* happened in those twenty years. He wasn't absent, and he wasn't asleep at the wheel. He was probably using it in ways I wasn't even seeing. But I also recognize that each unique detail of the journey was part of my story when I began sharing. It took a long time, yes, but he kept the vision in front of me that he's ultimately using it for good. And he's making good on that promise.

Several years ago, my pastor and friend Aaron Brockett said, "God cares way more about your availability than your ability." That one line taught me so much. It came in a season of heavy self-doubt around my *abilities*. In ministry, and I'm sure in your context too, it's sometimes easy for us to become enamored with the gifts and strengths we don't have. God has had to reconstruct my whole way of thinking around my heart and talents, and he used Aaron to help me see I need to be more focused on my *availability* and then God will make me able.

That's not super difficult to do in this conversation. *Lord, I have no idea how you want to use my story. I have no idea when you want to either. But I do know you want to, so I make myself available to you. Thank you for what you'll do.* Be available, be open, and the Lord will use us in a powerful way.

Ask Yourself

- Is there someone whose story has inspired you in your journey with mental health? What about their experience that has encouraged you to keep fighting?
- If you were to share your story of mental illness, how do you think people who know you best would react?
- Pray for one opportunity to share your testimony, and see how God answers that prayer.

CHAPTER SEVEN

THE POWER OF "EVEN IF"

If I could hear Christ praying for me in the next room, I would not fear a million enemies. Yet distance makes no difference. He is praying for me.

—Robert Murray McCheyne

I've been diagnosed with obsessive-compulsive disorder. In my experience, few people talk about the type of OCD that affects me. Most often I hear someone say in jest something like "that's the OCD in me" when they get distracted by a small detail or need something to be aligned or orderly. I get that it's a commonplace culturally to use the term more broadly, but all forms of OCD can be extremely debilitating.

OCD typically follows this pattern: obsessive thought, anxious reaction, and compulsive behavior. For me, OCD, in combination with illness anxiety disorder, created quite a mess. I could go from having a minor headache to a full-blown panic attack in a matter of *seconds* because my mind was just running ragged. My thoughts would go something like this: *My head hurts. Why? Maybe there's something wrong. Like, really wrong. I should look it up online to try to find some reassurance.*

It sounds ridiculous to write that—why would the Internet ever help in that situation? However, logic has no place when looking for a compulsive behavior to counter the obsessive thought. Sometimes my compulsive behavior would be asking people around me if they thought I was okay. Even reading the Bible and praying were compulsive behaviors for me. They weren't necessarily to grow closer to the Lord— they were instead efforts to get a quick hit to feel better.

This process was no different when my loved ones would feel sick. If one of my boys got ill, I would obsess and grow anxious around, thinking it could be something terrible. I would compulsively check their temperature or ask them how they were every three minutes. Whenever I did those things, I genuinely thought a positive answer or result would help. In reality, my mind was stuck in a cycle where the negativity would just repeat itself after a little bit. On and on, the cycle went.

I've explained this process before to people in the church, and unfortunately, I often left the conversation feeling like I was doing something wrong.

> *"Why are you afraid of something terrible happening? Just give that to Jesus."*

> *"Even if something terrible happens, God will take care of you."*

> *"Instead of searching the Internet for an answer, open up the Bible."*

> *"The Bible says fear not and don't be anxious—that's not what God wants for you."*

These sentiments aren't entirely wrong, and that's one of the reasons these conversations are so tricky in the church. Yes, God is faithful and can take care of my fears. Yes, the Bible has more hope than the Internet. Yes, I know I shouldn't be fearful. And yet I'm praying all the time, in scripture more than I've ever been, surrendering every single day to the Lordship of Christ, and if I feel a twinge in my stomach or my kids complain of any discomfort, I'm in a puddle literally in seconds.

I am so tired of the narrative that it's either/or with our faithfulness and pain. I now know it to be a both/and. After a few days of being on medicine to increase the serotonin in my brain, I felt like a completely different person. I had more of a buffer before the OCD train left the station. I could actually think *logically*. And for so many years, I avoided going this route because I bought into the lie that I needed to figure this out on my own, that it was an issue I could control.

When my struggles with anxiety became apparent, one of my first action steps was to memorize Philippians 4:6–9 (NLT): "Don't worry about anything; instead, pray about everything. Tell God what you need and thank him for all he has done. Then you will experience God's peace, which exceeds anything we can understand. His peace will guard your hearts and minds as you live in Christ Jesus. And now, dear brothers and sisters, one final thing. Fix your thoughts on what is true, and honorable, and right, and pure, and lovely, and admirable. Think about things that are excellent and worthy of praise. Keep putting into practice all you learned and received from me—everything you heard from me and saw me doing. Then the God of peace will be with you."

If you've struggled with your mental health and are a follower of Jesus, you've likely heard these verses. Maybe you've memorized them. Perhaps someone who has them memorized said them to you.

It's an incredible passage, but navigating it has been somewhat of a roller coaster for me. At first, I was all in. *Don't be anxious, don't be anxious, don't be anxious.* That momentum lasted about four hours. Then I realized it wasn't just about being anxious; instead, I should be replacing the anxiety with something—prayer. Got it. *Praying, praying, praying.*

I'm an enneagram one, and if you give me some suitable guardrails, I'll be off and running. As you can imagine, though, under the severe weight of anxiety and depression at times, this method didn't play out practically as I had hoped. Something wasn't working. In hindsight, I can see what some of those things were, but in the moment, I felt wrong for not being able to rid myself overnight of the anxiety. After years of studying this passage, I'm beginning to learn a few things about it.

First, when this passage plays out in life, it contains proof of Christianity. When you are under the weight and torment of anxiety and suddenly experience the God of peace, it truly goes beyond anything you could ever understand. And nothing else in this world can do that for us besides Jesus. This hope creates optimism in me, believing we're on the cusp of something extraordinary in this battle. We have seen and experienced something everyone in the world wants, and nobody can get anywhere else. We were made for peace, yet hardly any of us regularly have it. Peace is one of those things everyone understands, but you don't ever have to define it. We know when we see and feel it and when we don't.

In 2018, a poll was conducted with more than one hundred thousand people from fifteen different countries about the perception of peace worldwide.[4] One of the poll questions asked, "What would be most effective in creating long-term peace?" Instead of the answers involving security, political, and military intervention, the highest response was "Deal with reasons people fight in the first place." To have peace, we have to get to the root of the things keeping us from peace. And we follow a God that *promises* peace. If there's peace in our hearts and our

[4] chrome-extension://gphandlahdpffmccakmbngmbjnjiiahp/https://www.international-alert.org/wp-content/uploads/2021/08/Peace-Perceptions-Poll-XSum-EN-2018.pdf

minds, there will be peace throughout the world. We have access to a peace that surpasses understanding. Want to see a radically different world? Show it where to receive that kind of peace.

Second, I'm being reminded this passage says to bring our requests to God *with thanksgiving.* Sounds reminiscent of where Spurgeon was coming from. *Lord, thank you for my anxiety. I praise you in the midst of the depression.* It's what I've begun to know as the "even if" mindset. *Even if you choose not to heal me, you've done more for me than I could've ever imagined, and I will praise you.*

There were seasons when I pleaded with the Lord to take this from me just as Paul did. But this verse has shown me my pleading should be coupled with praise. I want to be thankful for every trial, and I've got a long way to go to get there. But some ground is being taken, and I pray the same for you.

Have you seen those billboards advertising lottery jackpots? I saw one the other day, and the number was astronomical. Spend a dollar, win seven hundred million. I began to daydream, and this might sound ridiculous, but what if someone came up to me and said, "Hey, so nobody won the jackpot, and we can't fit another digit on our fancy billboard. Do you want it?"

Here's the thing—I'd hesitate. Sure, it's a whole lot easier to say that knowing that question will never be asked of me. And I could do a lot of good with that money. A better pastor would immediately say yes and gift the whole thing to feed people in need worldwide.

However, I also know my propensity to seek comfort. And I know that, for me, being financially set and independent is somewhat of a scary prospect. I'm learning dependency is good for me. Maybe I've gone too far to the other extreme, but *I've seen my need for Jesus.* I don't want to do any of this without him. And I want my boys and the people I lead to see the same.

My third learning from Philippians 4:6–9 has happened through the Lord redeeming aspects of this passage for me. For several years, I've seen verses 8 and 9 be weaponized in the church and used to oversimplify a solution to anxiety. There were a lot of well-intentioned Christ followers, even close friends and coworkers, who would use this passage as a directive to me in times of struggle. "Aaron, don't be anxious, fix your thoughts on what's true."

And what was communicated in that was the experience I was going through wasn't true, that the feelings I had weren't true. I needed to simply remove the anxiety and replace it with God's truth. And what I think the enemy was doing through that was taking something subtle that isn't even entirely wrong, and he used it to press in on the shame I was already feeling. *Hey, Aaron, if you'd just think about what's true, you'd be good.* If you've never struggled with anxiety and depression, thanks for picking up this book! Also, please know I have never felt anything more real and more *true* than the weight of mental illness.

I remember at times my wife would reassure me, and she'd say, "Honey, you're okay, nothing is wrong, you're healthy, you're not failing, you're a great dad, you're a great husband."

And I remember vividly saying, "I would give anything to be able to believe that. I want so badly to know that those things are true. No matter how hard I try, I just can't feel what you're saying."

So a solution of fixing my eyes on what's true and that my "false" anxiety would evaporate was very hurtful and unhelpful. However, here's the subtlety in which the Lord has given me great peace. The truth I need to focus on is not that I'm not anxious. The truth that I need to focus on is in my anxiety, *he is still good*. He is sovereign. It doesn't surprise him, and he doesn't love me any less because of it. *And* he promises to redeem and use it in some way.

Learning that literally changed my life. *Lord, I feel these things, but you're still here, and you're still faithful, and I know you want to use this for your good.* My prayer life changed from prayers of shame like, "God, I'm sorry for not being able to see your truth," to prayers of hope like, "God, show me how you're going to use the truth of my pain for your good."

I've felt some of the weaponization of Philippians 4, but I've witnessed even more around the mentions of "fear not" in scripture. Depending on the translation you're referencing, this phrase appears a couple of hundred times in scripture. However, despite how it's been portrayed, it's not simply a command in scripture. *You're not supposed to fear, Aaron. You don't need to worry.* Okaaaaay. Now what?

That's why an accurate reading and interpretation of the Bible is so vital in this conversation because we might get half-truths if we're fully relying on someone else to tell us about God's words. We need to be examining it for ourselves.

Do you know what God often says when he's telling us we don't have to fear? *For I am with you.*

This isn't just some absent man up in the clouds telling us to stop everything we're doing. He's inviting us to something better—where we put our faith and trust in what he has for us instead of what only we can see. Philippians 4:8 tells us to fix our thoughts on the things that are true, noble, right, pure, lovely, admirable, excellent, and praiseworthy. It doesn't say to fix our thoughts on only the good parts of life. It's okay to acknowledge the reality of the trials we're in while thinking about the faithfulness of God to bring us through them.

Anyone struggling with anxiety and depression right now is likely asking two questions:

1. Will I feel like this forever?
2. How do I make it go away?

I still feel the weight of those questions like I was asking them yesterday. It feels so unsustainably hopeless when these are top of mind and even worse if the answers we come up with aren't helpful. Here's what Philippians 4 promises us we can take comfort in when these questions come to mind: *You will not feel like this forever—the God of perfect peace sees you, is with you, is for you, and will provide for you today and in each day to come.*

Will you pray for that type of peace today? If you're in a pit right now, pray it over your mind and your heart. If you know someone who is struggling today, pray it desperately over them. Pray it boldly, knowing victory is on our side. We are promised it. Revelation 21:1–5 (NLT) gives us a picture of the future to come:

> Then I saw a new heaven and a new earth, for the old heaven and the old earth had disappeared. And the sea was also gone. And I saw the holy city, the new Jerusalem, coming down from God out of heaven like a bride beautifully dressed for her husband. I heard a loud shout from the throne, saying, "Look, God's home is now among his people! He will live with them, and they will be his people. God himself will be with them. He will wipe every tear from their eyes, and there will be no more death or sorrow or crying or pain. All these things are gone forever." And the one sitting on the throne said, "Look, I am making everything new!" And then he said to me, "Write this down, for what I tell you is trustworthy and true."

Jesus is making all things new. Anticipate a day with no more tears, death, sorrow, or pain. As Spurgeon writes, "Christian, anticipate heaven … Within little time you will be rid of all your trials and your troubles." There were moments for me that felt like a day without trouble was a pipe dream. If you're in that place today, I get it. Read Revelation 21 over and over and over again until a part of his peace washes over you. I promise, your suffering is not permanent.

Ask Yourself

- How do you feel about medically treating mental illness? What influences or sources have informed your beliefs on this topic?
- What do you think if means to give your fears to God? How does that look practically?
- Do you try to deal with your mental illness on your own? How might depending on others and depending on Jesus help you in your struggle?

CHAPTER EIGHT

DESIRING HEAVEN VERSUS CONSIDERING SUICIDE

If someone ever comes at you with the lie that God can't be in the midst of your depression, or it wouldn't be happening if you had more faith, guide them to Job 7:1–21 (NLT):

> *Is not all human life a struggle? Our lives are like that of a hired hand, like a worker who longs for the shade, like a servant waiting to be paid. I, too, have been assigned months of futility, long and weary nights of misery. Lying in bed, I think, "When will it be morning?" But the night drags on, and I toss till dawn. My body is covered with maggots and scabs. My skin breaks open, oozing with pus. My days fly faster than a weaver's shuttle. They end without hope.*
>
> *O God, remember that my life is but a breath, and I will never again feel happiness. You see me now, but not for long. You will look for me, but I will be gone. Just as a cloud dissipates and vanishes, those who die will not come back. They are gone forever from their home—never to be*

seen again. I cannot keep from speaking. I must express my anguish. My bitter soul must complain. Am I a sea monster or a dragon that you must place me under guard? I think, "My bed will comfort me, and sleep will ease my misery," but then you shatter me with dreams and terrify me with visions. I would rather be strangled—rather die than suffer like this. I hate my life and don't want to go on living. Oh, leave me alone for my few remaining days.

What are people, that you should make so much of us, that you should think of us so often? For you examine us every morning and test us every moment. Why won't you leave me alone, at least long enough for me to swallow! If I have sinned, what have I done to you, O watcher of all humanity? Why make me your target? Am I a burden to you? Why not just forgive my sin and take away my guilt? For soon I will lie down in the dust and die. When you look for me, I will be gone.

Has there been a more candid admission of depression than this?

- *I will never again feel happiness.*
- *I must express my anguish.*
- *My bitter soul must complain.*
- *I would rather be strangled—rather die than suffer like this.*
- *I hate my life and don't want to go on living.*
- *Why make me your target?*

When we find ourselves in the most profound state of depression and uttering words like these, we have a companion in Job. He was suffering greatly and blaming God for it. He had no vision for the future that awaited him. He had no hope.

Have you been there? I pray you haven't. Unfortunately, I remember my rock bottom like it was yesterday. I was lying in bed one morning and couldn't imagine waking up for the day. I was overwhelmed by even the prospect of standing up and felt like I had nothing to give.

I tried articulating this feeling to Megan and told her the best time of day was when I was asleep because there was no attack then. My best times weren't laughing with her and the kids. It wasn't on date nights with her. The scary thing was I didn't have to think about this for a second before saying it. I knew the time of no attack when I was removed from reality. Sleep was the only time without pain.

It was a sobering conversation. She cried. I cried. She didn't try to fix me; she just sat with me in the weight of that. I was scared, she was scared, but we were together. Megan is beautiful, funny, and brilliant—but the thing I admire most is her courage. Moments like this, where she seemed to lean into the difficulties, are so humbling to reflect on.

One of the aims of this book is to speak as candidly as possible. Even as we discuss challenging, complex parts of the conversation on mental health, there's one aspect trickier than any—suicide. How is a follower of Jesus to navigate this appropriately? Let's look at some of the tensions that exist here:

- We were made *with* purpose *for* a purpose. We were created in God's image to be in a relationship with him and to do whatever we can to get his kids back to him. There's a reason we're alive on earth.

- We are told this isn't our home. We are *in* the world, not *of* the world. Heaven is perfect, and our hope is placed in eternity, not in this life.

75

- We should idolize God and God only, not the things of this world. Yet we're surrounded by the world while having to wait for perfect harmony with God in heaven.
- We don't have explicit references to God's view of suicide in scripture but know that God condemns murder and that each scriptural reference of suicide is not affirmed as God's will.

There are also unwritten aspects of this conversation many of us are carrying around. For some reason, I have always felt incredible shame associated with suicide.

When I was a kid and first heard of someone in the church dying by suicide, I assumed they weren't a Christian after all. Looking back, I have no idea where that came from, but something from my background informed that view. Or I was born with that assumption, and nothing taught me differently. Either way, I was wrong. But I know I'm not alone in the feelings of confusion around this topic in the church. There are a lot of tensions here.

I've shared being alone physically has been a particular challenge for my mental health at times. I remember one day on vacation when I felt a significant, thick weight that had been growing for weeks.

I was in the shower, alone in my thoughts, and I remember wanting to be relieved of the pain so badly. I had one of those conversations with God where I was candid about what I was feeling, and I let him know, if he wanted to take me right then, I was good with it. Maybe I should always be good with it through a heavenly perspective, but at this moment, it was out of total surrender and desperation that I let him know I wanted to be in heaven more than on earth. He didn't zap me up despite my permission and has kept me in the game for much longer. I'm incredibly grateful for that.

Have you ever met someone who has a phenomenal eternal

perspective? Like they're not at all attached to this world? Based on Colossians 3:2 (ESV), that's probably something we all should strive for. "Set your minds on things that are above, not on things that are on earth."

When I was in my early twenties, I had a coworker named Sonni who served as a missionary to unreached people groups across the world. When he turned fifty, I wished him a happy birthday, and he turned to me with the biggest smile and said, "One year closer to heaven!"

It was the most genuine response, and I immediately recognized I wanted more of that. More times than not, I haven't had that perspective. I think I have a healthy love of the people around me and the calling God has placed on my life. But at times I *really* want to stay here. Unfortunately, the closest I've been to a genuine heavenly longing is under the weight of mental illness.

The perfect balance of these perspectives is found on a very thin line somewhere right in the middle. We should long for heaven to be united with Jesus. A future of eternal joy and painlessness awaits us—praise God. And we shouldn't take it upon ourselves to get there any sooner than God intends. While we're on earth, we have a purpose. Every day, in any pain, we can make a difference for his kingdom.

Paul captures this balance so eloquently in 2 Corinthians 1:3–11 (ESV). He describes a desire to be rescued from the intense suffering he had experienced and, in the same breath, points to a dependence on Christ that he will sustain, rescue, and continue to use Paul. It's the perspective we all should be aiming for.

> *Blessed be the God and Father of our Lord Jesus Christ,*
> *the Father of mercies and God of all comfort, who comforts*
> *us in all our affliction, so that we may be able to comfort*
> *those who are in any affliction, with the comfort with*

which we ourselves are comforted by God. For as we share abundantly in Christ's sufferings, so through Christ we share abundantly in comfort too. If we are afflicted, it is for your comfort and salvation; and if we are comforted, it is for your comfort, which you experience when you patiently endure the same sufferings that we suffer. Our hope for you is unshaken, for we know that as you share in our sufferings, you will also share in our comfort. For we do not want you to be unaware, brothers, of the affliction we experienced in Asia. For we were so utterly burdened beyond our strength that we despaired of life itself. Indeed, we felt that we had received the sentence of death. But that was to make us rely not on ourselves but on God who raises the dead. He delivered us from such a deadly peril, and he will deliver us. On him we have set our hope that he will deliver us again. You also must help us by prayer, so that many will give thanks on our behalf for the blessing granted us through the prayers of many.

Can you relate with Paul? *So utterly burdened beyond our strength that we despaired of life itself.* I've been there; in over my head, feeling the weight of the world, and desperately wanting relief. And I've had to remind myself God allowed that sentence in *his* word. In 2 Timothy, it says all of scripture is God-breathed, and we see this beautiful vulnerability from Paul to convey a cycle many of us are very familiar with—suffering, hopelessness, rescue, hope, and a perspective toward the future that the battle is ongoing, but victory is ultimately on our side.

Sometimes I just need to know I'm not alone in trying to find this balance. As much as it pains me that others are experiencing what I have gone through, I also take so much comfort in knowing it's a group effort to keep fighting. If I am the only person struggling to long for heaven and staying committed to earth, what a lonely place to be. But I'm not. And neither are you.

Spurgeon writes, "Death would be welcomed as a relief by those whose depressed spirits make their existence a living death. Are good men ever permitted to suffer thus? Indeed they are; and some of them are even all their lifetime subject to bondage. O Lord, Be pleased to set free thy prisoners of hope! Let none of thy mourners imagine that a strange thing has happened unto him, but rather rejoice as he sees the footprints of brethren who have trodden this desert before."[5]

If I had to guess, some of you reading this today are under such terrible anguish that you are considering taking your life. Please find encouragement in these words that many have trodden through this desert before and *survived*.

Job has walked this path before. Paul has walked this path before. Spurgeon has walked this path before. I have walked this path before, and I commit to you that I'll keep walking. We must stay in the game, keep fighting, and prove to one another we can be victorious in the battle on this side of eternity.

Here are some practical things to do today if you're struggling to find this balance:

Talk to Someone

Please don't suffer alone. It's not worth it, and it's not necessary. There are some great resources in the last chapter of this book that I would recommend, but it doesn't have to be anything on that list. Just do not go at this alone. Talk to a doctor, a

---

[5] https://archive.spurgeon.org/treasury/ps088.php

therapist, a family member, a friend, a coworker, or a total stranger. It may not go as planned, but just get that elephant off your chest and begin to invite others in. At some point, someone will wrap their arms around you.

Lock In on Your Why

What's your purpose? Despite the noise you may be hearing, you absolutely have a purpose. For me, it's my three boys— Wesley, Abram, and Roman. I'm staying in the fight for them. I don't know what they will struggle with in life, but one thing is guaranteed: They will have trials. On my worst, lowest days, I know my fight will inspire them to do the same at some point in their life. Just like the trials of others are being redeemed in my life, I believe my pain will continue to be redeemed in their lives. That's motivating for me.

Be Relentless in Your Pursuit of Jesus

Suicidal ideation is not a sin; it's a byproduct of overwhelm. But it's not the finish line Jesus has for you. In Matthew 11:28–30 (NLT), he says, "Come to me, all of you who are weary and carry heavy burdens, and I will give you rest. Take my yoke upon you. Let me teach you, because I am humble and gentle at heart, and you will find rest for your souls. For my yoke is easy to bear, and the burden I give you is light."

If you don't have a daily quiet time in his word, begin one. If you don't have a regular rhythm of prayer, make one. For followers of Jesus, these should be non-negotiables in the battle for mental health. Time with the Lord may start as a discipline for you—something you've got to really grind to make happen. Eventually, you won't be able to imagine life without it.

Our office has a breakroom that often gets filled with leftover treats from ministry events; first come, first served. My office is just down the hall, and I pass by the room probably ten to twenty times a day, and for some reason, the best doughnuts in our city continue to show up there. Three to five years ago, I wouldn't pass a good doughnut up. Now, after countless afternoons of my stomach writhing in pain, it's really easy to look the other way.

I've experienced life without proximity to Jesus. In all honesty, it's not great. I've had him as an add-on instead of the main event, and it's so unfulfilling. Now I'm desperate for my time with him in the morning. I go to bed looking forward to waking up. It's a stark contrast from a few years ago, and there are many reasons for that. However, prioritizing my time with him daily has been so rewarding.

Psalm 119:105 (NIV) says, "Your word is a lamp for my feet, a light on my path." If you are walking through your darkest moments, talk to him. We're not meant to navigate the dark without his light. Find refuge in him today.

Ask Yourself

- Is there any part of Job's story that you can relate to? How does reading Job 7 make you feel?
- Who can you talk with today?
- What's your purpose? This doesn't need to be grand or elaborate, just name something that you know you were created for.
- What can you do to run toward Jesus with everything you've got today?

CHAPTER NINE

THE STIGMAS OF MENTAL ILLNESS VERSUS GOD'S WORD

Herein lies one of the most pervasive misunderstandings regarding mental illness: that God spares this kind of pain and suffering from those with deep and abiding faith. All too often, the assumption in the church is that those who continue to suffer from mental illness lack sufficient faith.
—Stephen Grcevich, MD, *Mental Health and the Church: A Ministry Handbook for Including Children and Adults with ADHD, Anxiety, Mood Disorders, and Other Common Mental Health Conditions*

To make a difference in the conversation on mental health, we have to face several stigmas that have infiltrated the conversation. A stigma is defined as a mark of disgrace or infamy, a stain or reproach, on one's reputation.[6] Unfortunately, the church isn't exempt from these. Rather, I believe the stigmas Christians face are some of the worst to contend

---

[6] https://www.dictionary.com/browse/stigma

with in the conversation. A non-exhaustive list would look something like this:

- Mental illness is a sign of weakness.
- Mental illness is a sin issue.
- Mental illness needs to be surrendered to Jesus, and he will take care of it.
- Mental illness should just be prayed away.
- Mental illness only affects people who don't have enough faith.
- Mental illness is just a sign of being tested.

That's a tough list to write and read, not because any of it is true, but because it brings to mind the conversations I've heard each of these sentiments. And it highlights what I know some people are hearing right now.

I hate to say it, but there were seasons when I believed some of these stigmas. As part of the enemy's plan to lie and deceive me into thinking I was too far gone, he tried to convince me my illness was (1) easily solvable and (2) my fault.

Unfortunately, he often used God's people to press in on that deception. Sharing about my struggle has never been easy, but it's been most difficult when Christians have made me feel less because of what I'm enduring.

I'm so grateful to see the situation more clearly now. And that's only happened because of the comfort and clarity the Bible has provided me.

I want to speak to each of these stigmas, but I don't want to use my words alone to do so—I want to use God's words. The reasoning for that might seem obvious, but it's often been helpful to remind myself of the "why" of God's word, especially in seasons when I'm struggling. I love the imagery God provides in Ephesians 6 of the armor he has given to his followers. Why would someone need armor? Because they're going into battle. And mental illness is a battle not for the ill-prepared. Therefore, he's given us

- The belt of truth
- The breastplate of righteousness
- The shoes of peace
- The shield of faith
- The helmet of salvation
- The sword of the spirit

I've never fought in a legitimate physical battle, so I'm no expert on armor. However, unless we're in some MMA/helmet-butting altercation, we have only one offensive weapon on this list. It's described in Ephesians 6:17 (NLT) as "the sword of the Spirit, which is the word of God."

Why six items for defense, with the sword serving a dual purpose, and one for offense? If I'm preparing my kids for a battle, I will load so many things onto them that they may be unable to walk out the door. The disparity tells me a couple of things.

First, we need a ton of armor to protect us because we'll take a lot of shots. Jesus affirmed in Matthew 7:13–14 (ESV), "Enter by the narrow gate. For the gate is wide and the way is easy that leads to destruction, and those who enter by it are many. For the gate is narrow and the way is hard that leads to life, and those who find it are few." That's not specific to mental illness, but Jesus consistently said following him will bring difficulties. *The way is hard.* So he's equipped us with the armor to defend ourselves.

Second, he gives us just one thing for offense because he knows it's sufficient. His word is all we need. This simplifies our attack so much for us. Instead of learning to fire several different weapons and involve every limb we have in that attack, he gives us one sword to achieve victory.

His word is more than enough. So to counter the stigmas above, let's look at the scriptures that do just that.

Stigma 1: Mental illness is a sign of weakness.

And what's your point? Similar to the word "brokenness," there's a misunderstanding of the Christian walk if "weakness" is seen as a negative thing.

I was born in the late '80s and have pushed back regularly to the perception that men should be this strong, unbreakable, everything-but-weak type of person. Nah, I don't want any of that. I know I'm weak, and I'm grateful for it. I've felt the weight of the world and know I can't carry all that on my own.

I had someone I love and respect dearly tell me as a compliment, "Aaron, you're the weakest person I know. And therefore, you're one of the strongest people I know." I was really grateful for the second sentence because I did not see the compliment at first. At some points in my life, hearing I was extremely weak would have wrecked me. But after the season I've walked through, it is music to my ears.

So many passages affirm this:

> 2 Corinthians 12:7–10 (NLT): "To keep me from becoming proud, I was given a thorn in my flesh, a messenger from Satan to torment me and keep me from becoming proud. Three different times I begged the Lord to take it away. Each time he said, 'My grace is all you need. My power works best in weakness.' So now I am glad to boast about my weaknesses, so that the power of Christ can work through me. That's why I take pleasure in my weaknesses, and in the insults,

hardships, persecutions, and troubles that I suffer for Christ. For when I am weak, then I am strong."

Romans 8:26 (NLT): "And the Holy Spirit helps us in our weakness. For example, we don't know what God wants us to pray for. But the Holy Spirit prays for us with groanings that cannot be expressed in words."

Isaiah 40:29 (NLT): "He gives power to the weak and strength to the powerless."

Philippians 4:13 (NLT): "For I can do everything through Christ, who gives me strength."

Stigma 2: Mental illness is a sin issue.

Throughout scripture, people make mistakes. It's kind of a cornerstone of the gospel message. God created everything and did so perfectly. People messed it up. God redeemed it all through Jesus. There isn't much gray in the Bible when it comes to calling sin what it is. So this stigma is pretty baffling. There isn't a single example in scripture of anxiety or depression being called a sin.

We've mentioned Moses and David and the mental struggles they had to overcome. In response to these moments of struggle, God often encourages or realigns the perspectives of these men. However, when dealing with sin issues they experienced, a simple realignment was *never* God's approach. In fact, we see in Numbers 20, when Moses commits the sin of disobedience, God bans him from entering the promised land. And in 2 Samuel 11, God allows David's son to die after David commits adultery. God has always dealt swiftly with sin. But with mental and physical illness, he doesn't punish. Instead, he comforts.

The story of the prophet Elijah in 1 Kings 18 and 19 is another example of God's response when we are at our lowest points.

In chapter 18, Elijah finds himself in a head-to-head contest with 450 prophets of the false god Baal. Yes, 450 against one. The contest stems from a disagreement over which is real—God or Baal. It's decided whichever one can create fire first must be a real god. For many hours, the false prophets attempt to conjure up a fire through Baal but have no success. When it's Elijah's turn, the Lord is immediately victorious and then he helps Elijah kill all 450 false prophets.

Moments later, Elijah's life is threatened by Queen Jezebel. Anxiety takes over Elijah at that moment. Despite the Lord's victory for Elijah over hundreds of people that same day, this threat hits home, and Elijah flees to the wilderness and prays he would die in verse 4: "I have had enough, Lord," he said. "Take my life, for I am no better than my ancestors who have already died" (1 Kings 19:4 NLT).

I've been there. I will watch God move mountains, do the miraculous, and then wonder how I will get out of a small pickle—all on the same day. And if that pressure and anxiety was a sin, then I think we'd see a different response from God than what we see with Elijah in this story. The Lord doesn't strike him dead. He doesn't require him to stop serving. Instead, he gives Elijah even more responsibility in overseeing another prophet and sends him out to continue his ministry.

Stigma 3: Mental illness needs to be surrendered to Jesus, and he will take care of it.

Ah, so close—I agree with the first part. We need to surrender any type of anguish to Jesus immediately. However, the word *surrender* implies an inherent lack of control, so by surrendering something, we're opening ourselves up to the possibility it won't simply be taken care of.

Surrender is defined as "to give oneself up, as into the power of another; submit or yield."[7]

If we surrender our mental illness over to the Lord, as we all should in some way, then we are giving up that we have anything to do with the result. Surrendering admits the possibility that the battle might stick around. But it's no longer up to us, and Jesus will see it through.

Instead of immediate relief from pain, scripture paints a picture of an ongoing battle, a battle in which we need the Lord to uphold us, strengthen us, and provide endurance for us.

> Isaiah 41:10 (ESV): "Fear not, for I am with you; be not dismayed, for I am your God; I will strengthen you, I will help you, I will uphold you with my righteous right hand."

> Romans 8:31 (ESV): "What then shall we say to these things? If God is for us, who can be against us?"

> Romans 8:18 (ESV): "For I consider that the sufferings of this present time are not worth comparing with the glory that is to be revealed to us."

Let's surrender these trials to him daily. But let's not oversimplify that surrender is equal to relief. Not at all the same.

Stigma 4: Mental illness should just be prayed away.

Illness, in general, should be prayed about, yes. Whether it goes away is outside of our control. We should constantly be praying just as 1 Thessalonians 5:17 (ESV) tells us, to "pray without ceasing."

---

[7] https://www.dictionary.com/browse/surrender

Also, whenever and wherever we need God, we absolutely need to be devoted to prayer. I believe wholeheartedly my prayers where I pleaded for healing were granted through doctors, people, and medicine. The Lord's hand was all over that. But again, prayer isn't a way for us to simply get a positive answer for a need we have. That's entirely under the control of the Lord, and prayer is the act of surrendering our needs to him.

Pray for victory. Don't allow this stigma to change how you see prayer. As we see in his word, prayer is critical and a necessary part of our walk with the Lord.

> 1 John 5:14 (NLT): "And we are confident that he hears us whenever we ask for anything that pleases him."

> Ephesians 6:18 (NLT): "Pray in the Spirit at all times and on every occasion. Stay alert and be persistent in your prayers for all believers everywhere."

> Job 22:27 (NIV): "You will pray to him, and he will hear you, and you will fulfill your vows to him."

> Jeremiah 29:12 (NLT): "In those days when you pray, I will listen."

> James 5:13 (NLT): "Are any of you suffering hardships? You should pray. Are any of you happy? You should sing praises."

> Mark 11:24 (NLT) "I tell you, you can pray for anything, and if you believe that you've received it, it will be yours."

Stigma 5: Mental illness only affects people who don't have enough faith.

I would contend the most extraordinary faith comes from illness. To suffer personally from either mental or physical ailments *and still believe* in God's goodness requires deep, intimate faith. I've seen my greatest faith come in my most difficult times. The times when I'm thriving are the times when I've sensed waning proximity to the Lord.

In Hebrews 4, God gives us a list of people who demonstrated remarkable faith throughout scripture. In this list, we see the aforementioned David and Moses, who had great mental trials but ultimately persevered and grew in their faith. There's also Joshua, whom the Lord encouraged to be strong and courageous; and Sarah and Abraham, who struggled to wait for God's promise that an enormous legacy would stem from their family tree.

Struggle isn't reserved for people with little faith. As we see throughout scripture, the two absolutely coexist.

Stigma 6: Mental illness is just a sign of being tested.

Anecdotally, this is the least-referenced stigma I've heard on this list, but I think it's a general oversimplification. Every struggle is, in some way, a test, I suppose. But this sounds pretty dismissive, and mental illness is anything but dismissive. Scripture speaks a lot about testing and is clear that trials will develop our character if we allow them to.

> Job 23:10 (ESV): "But he knows the way that I take; when he has tried me, I shall come out as gold."

> 1 Corinthians 10:13 (ESV): "No temptation has overtaken you that is not common to man. God is

faithful, and he will not let you be tempted beyond your ability, but with the temptation he will also provide the way of escape, that you may be able to endure it."

Psalm 66:8–12 (ESV): "Bless our God, O peoples; let the sound of his praise be heard, who has kept our soul among the living and has not let our feet slip. For you, O God, have tested us; you have tried us as silver is tried. You brought us into the net; you laid a crushing burden on our backs; you let men ride over our heads; we went through fire and through water; yet you have brought us out to a place of abundance."

James 1:3 (ESV): "For you know that the testing of your faith produces steadfastness."

James 1:12 (NLT): "God blesses those who patiently endure testing and temptation. Afterward they will receive the crown of life that God has promised to those who love him."

I hope you walk away from this chapter better armed to combat the noise you may be experiencing. These scripture references are just scratching the surface of God's encouragement for you. Here's what I want you to know more than anything before you go to the next chapter: When held up to God's word, the stigmas that exist in the conversation on mental health are entirely bogus. They're not true. Your mental illness does not define you, and you certainly aren't any less of a person because of it. God's word is a refuge, and I pray you devour it in this season and in the months and years to come. It is an invaluable weapon in the war and is readily available to us daily.

Ask Yourself

- Which stigma about mental illness hits you hardest? Which stigma has affected you most?
- Which stigma do you see regularly, and how can you help counter it?
- What passage in the Bible do you need to lean into more in the coming weeks?

CHAPTER TEN

LEANING IN VERSUS SPIRITUAL WARFARE

You live in a world at war. Spiritual attack must be a category you think in or you will misunderstand more than half of what happens in your marriage.
—John Eldredge, *Love and War: Finding the Marriage You've Dreamed Of*

While being trained to facilitate premarital counseling in our church, one line caught me off guard when I first heard it: "Satan hates your marriage, and he wants it to fail."

Yeesh, isn't there a nicer way to say that? Whether the delivery of that line is a little brash, I can't argue with the truth. If I believe what the Bible says about heaven, hell, God, and Satan, then there's no way to kindly say how the enemy views our relationships. All relationships, romantic or not, are designed by God to bring glory to him. The enemy's attack on relationships then should not surprise us. And by acknowledging it proactively, we can hopefully be aware of the instances where an attack is prevalent.

This part of the battle has never been more prominent than when navigating mental health crises. Despite Megan and I knowing neither of us was to blame for our situation, we weren't always on the same page. Sometimes she was frustrated we weren't maximizing our time together. Sometimes I was frustrated because she didn't fully know what I was experiencing. We didn't want to be in our situation, and we would've given anything to get out of it. That tension weighed on our marriage.

In May 2020, we were celebrating our eleventh anniversary. The world was still very much shut down because of the COVID-19 pandemic, but we had planned a great night, including a carry-out from a favorite restaurant and a movie at home.

On many of our anniversaries, we'd talk about our favorite memories or things we were looking forward to. This was an excellent opportunity to do just that with a third boy on the way in just a couple of weeks. There was only one issue—my mind was a mess. I had been having problems with acid reflux for a while, and my struggle with illness anxiety disorder was beginning to spin up into a panic. I couldn't swallow food without thinking about it. What started as anxiety about acid reflux quickly turned into obsessive-compulsive thoughts about stomach cancer and other worst-case scenarios.

Have you ever had high expectations for something, only for it to fall drastically short? That's the best way to summarize our anniversary dinner that year. We ate and talked, but we mostly cried. Through tears, we wished the burden would be lifted and things could return to "normal." Megan articulated she felt life was on hold. I then shared how that comment brushed up against the lie I had been told several months before that I was holding our family back. We were bleeding out all over each other.

But in that conversation and every other one, we had a choice to make. Were we going to be offended? Were we going to fight for each other or just fight each other? Were we going to lean into the discomfort and the pain, or were we going to run? Thankfully, we knew the enemy wanted this to separate us. We knew our boys were worse off if we didn't push through it. And so we never considered another option—we kept communicating and working. I'm so grateful we did.

In his book *The Four Loves*, C. S. Lewis said, "To love at all is to be vulnerable. Love anything, and your heart will be wrung and possibly broken. If you want to make sure of keeping it intact, you must give it to no one, not even an animal. Wrap it carefully round with hobbies and little luxuries; avoid all entanglements. Lock it up safe in the casket or coffin of your selfishness. But in that casket, safe, dark, motionless, airless, it will change. It will not be broken; it will become unbreakable, impenetrable, irredeemable. To love is to be vulnerable."[8]

From my perspective, loving Megan best meant I had to be as vulnerable as possible. It hurt so badly to tell Megan how I was doing because I knew I risked disappointing her. It's easier to say "I'm great!" than to acknowledge how bad I feel. I learned to bring her into where my mind was at was to invite her into the sadness. As much as I didn't want that for her, I wanted to allow her to be closer to me than try to protect her from me. So every time we spoke, we intentionally decided to be vulnerable. That was more difficult than glossing over how we felt, but we knew it'd be worth it.

Seeing a dysfunctional marriage growing up taught me how vital healthy communication is. Often what appears to be a different issue altogether is a communication gap. Some couples face financial problems, but many couples are actually just not communicating well about their finances. Some marriages face intimacy issues, but many simply are not discussing sex how they should. Megan and I could've said we were having issues around my mental health, but really, the only

---

[8] *The Four Loves* by C. S. Lewis © 1960 C. S. Lewis Pte. Ltd.

problem was whether we would communicate openly about it. We had, and continue to have, a choice to make.

None of it is easy, however. And we're all in different places right now, dealing with varying pain points in this conversation. You might find yourself in one of these situations right now:

- Struggling with mental illness and feeling like a burden to your supportive family
- Struggling with mental illness and not receiving the support you think you need
- Supporting someone in your family who is struggling with mental illness and you're feeling tired, overwhelmed, sad, or disappointed
- Wanting to support someone in your family who is in need but you don't know where to start or what to do

Please know you're not alone, regardless of where you're at. Megan and I have found ourselves in each category at various times. I know you can be made to feel like you're alone—that's one of the enemy's main tactics. But you're not. We stand with you.

If you're struggling with your mental health and need more support or currently feel like a burden, don't give in to the temptation to isolate. Family support is critical for you. However, find the right amount to give to your family and find other outlets as well.

I told Megan everything, but I also used discernment in what I asked her to take on in the battle. I needed a doctor to work with me on some things. I needed a counselor to work with me on other things. And I needed other men I could be in the trenches with. In some seasons, I confided in all these people exceptionally well, and there were times when I could've done much better. But it was a rhythm I knew I needed to maintain, not to put all the weight on Megan.

If you're a family member of someone who is carrying a heavy mental burden right now, please receive these three words—*we see you*. Your situation is likely very different from your expectations, and your courage to continue pressing on is making a difference. You might not have a line of sight to the fruit this season will produce, but I assure you it will happen. Megan's resilience over the last several years has cultivated fruit for her, me, our boys, and many who have heard our story. You don't need a specific platform to have an impact—people are watching you who will be inspired by your love, courage, and perseverance.

In John 13:34–35 (NIV), Jesus says, "A new command I give you: love one another. As I have loved you, so you must love one another. By this everyone will know that you are my disciples, if you love one another."

Megan is such a picture of Christ to me as has been the case throughout our marriage. When in labor with our first son, Wesley, she opted for a last-minute cesarean section because the dude measured large—like really, really large. When her options were to choose what was safest for Wesley or what was best for her, she didn't hesitate to pick him. She's done the same as I've dealt with mental health issues. She would tell you she hasn't done it perfectly, but I would say perfect isn't even the goal. She's been such a gift to me in the way she's loved me unconditionally and has continued to show up and lean in. And I know it's making an impact on people as we speak.

I was recently part of a retreat alongside a couple of dozen men and was asked, "What do you need courage for right now?" As I wrote this book, I shared I could use courage to sign Megan and me back up for some additional spiritual warfare. Coming out of the season we've been in, that isn't easy to get excited about. But I'm resolved this is what the Lord is asking us to do, and he will provide a way through all of it. And I truly believe this project isn't just mine, but Megan and I are mutually carrying this. As we navigate life together, highs and lows affect us, and going more public with this battle means we're engaging with it at another level.

Loving, serving, and prioritizing others sounds (and is) great, but the reality is caregivers also need a ton of support in this battle. That's not always easy to get sometimes because we don't know where to go for it. Also, the stigmas we've unpacked don't only apply to people struggling with their mental health—they're also quite relevant for the caregivers. *What will people think of my husband/wife if they find out about their struggle? What will people say about my parenting if they know my kid is struggling?*

For the caregiver's health, we must create safe spaces for these situations to be processed. There are relational needs that must be met, and they won't be unless we encourage the conversation to happen in the first place.

Megan and I each have a personal lens on the role of the caregiver/companion. She played that role, so her perspective is unique and invaluable. I have been the beneficiary of her being in that role, so there are certain things that have stood out to me as well over the last several years. Together, we want to expand on our perspectives and provide some words of advice for anyone supporting someone with mental health struggles.

From Megan:

Stop Talking—Start Listening

I've been learning this lesson on multiple fronts. I help lead a small group of other women, and this is highly relevant there too. I need to resist the urge to provide a Band-Aid solution or immediately point them to a Bible verse I think would turn things around for them. Instead of thinking a compelling response is needed, I've realized sometimes people simply need me to sit with them, to truly sit with what they're going through and be present. I don't need to try and reason any of their struggles away for them. It does more harm than good when I attempt to do that.

Affirm Feelings Even If They Don't Make Sense to You

There's often a big difference between what we want to provide and what someone else needs. It's so important to determine the real need that someone else has and attempt to meet *that*. Many people who are struggling for mental health need affirmation and validation of what they're going through. They need a reminder that it's okay to feel this way. What they often don't need is for us to try to compare our situation with theirs.

Make sure they know how much you appreciate they shared it with you in the first place. Encourage their strength to be vulnerable and how unique that is right now. Give them the courage to keep talking about it and to keep going.

Tell Them Way Too Much about Your Love for Them

This might be more specific to mine and Aaron's situation, but I'd guess it's still relevant for many who are struggling. Knowing the lie Aaron was hearing—that he was holding us back—it's been top of mind for me to combat that whenever I can. I want him to know unequivocally how much he's loved, needed, accepted, desired, and appreciated. I've tried to do that verbally and with my actions. In his darkest moments, when the volume is turned up, I want him to be able to hear my voice, reminding him of how much better he makes our family. I want there to be no room for doubt over that truth.

From Aaron:

Ask for Help

You're not expected to carry this weight on your own. Reach out to a friend and share a relational need you have. Talk with a counselor, pray with a pastor, e-mail or call some of the resources toward the end of this book. Whatever you do, avoid the unrelenting pressure to be superhuman. So many of us have your back. Let us help.

Stay Compassionate

As you continue to navigate situations with your loved one, fight to keep a heart of compassion. The person struggling with mental health didn't choose this, nor did you. That means there needs to be an inordinate amount of grace extended toward both of you. You're not wrong for being frustrated with the situation. But do everything you can to stay sweet in the midst of it.

Also, show yourself compassion. You'll drop some balls and make some mistakes—it's inevitable. But you are making a monumental difference in this battle. Try not to be discouraged by the things you wish you were doing better.

Don't Neglect Yourself

Being selfless doesn't mean we don't take care of ourselves. However, that's a common error we can make in pursuing humility and serving others. If you are caring for or supporting someone who is struggling with mental illness, it's critical you're at your best. That's going to mean doing some things that probably feel incredibly selfish to you. I've almost needed to ban Megan from home sometimes to get her to take a break. She will serve the four of us from morning to midnight without the reminder to do what she needs.

There's a lot of wisdom in this principle we find in the life and ministry of Jesus. In Mark 6:31 (NLT), after the apostles return from a lengthy trip, Jesus says to them, "Let's go off by ourselves to a quiet place and rest awhile." They could've met many more needs at the time, but he knew they needed to be refreshed. Jesus also modeled this in his life, often retreating to be filled up, grieve, discern, and pray.

If the perfect example of humility and servant-leadership knew to take a break for himself, then we absolutely need to as well. *Self-care is not selfish.* If we are intentional about getting refreshed, then the people around us will get a healthier and better version of us as opposed to the alternative—a burned-out version of ourselves.

Megan and I understand every situation is unique, and we wouldn't want to overapply these principles. However, these have been fundamental as we've learned to walk through this season together. At times we've felt alone because of the burden being carried. If you feel that way today, whether you are battling mental illness or you're in a support role, we want you to know you're not on your own. We see you. We stand with you. We are praying for you and fighting with you.

Ask Yourself

- How does understanding Satan's tactics and desires influence the way you see conflict in relationships?
- What do we stand to lose by being vulnerable? What do we stand to gain?
- Does one of the following describe you best right now:
  - o Struggling with mental illness and feeling like a burden to your supportive family
  - o Struggling with mental illness and not receiving the support you think you need
  - o Supporting someone in your family who is struggling with mental illness and you're feeling tired, overwhelmed, sad, or disappointed
  - o Wanting to support someone in your family who is in need but you don't know where to start or what to do

- What's something you can do this week to care for yourself?

CHAPTER ELEVEN

IT'S NOT FAITH VERSUS MEDICINE

No one would ever say that someone with a broken arm or a broken leg is less than a whole person, but people say that or imply that all the time about people with mental illness.
—Elyn R. Saks, 2007

The first time I was prescribed an antidepressant, I had just filled out a five-question survey on an iPad in front of a physician's assistant. I made that appointment after a weekend when my illness anxiety disorder was running rampant.

Megan was pregnant and given an at-home blood pressure monitor, and for some reason, I put that on and set off an OCD cycle of an intensity I had never experienced before. The first reading was *slightly* high. That happened on a Friday afternoon, and without the opportunity to consult a doctor over the weekend, I just *kept* taking readings to try to give myself some peace. Unsurprisingly, those attempts never worked, and my stress just made each reading go higher.

One night I said good night to my boys, and I fell asleep crying, believing it was the last time I'd see them because I thought I was on the verge of a heart attack because of the readings I was seeing. It was horrifying.

When I finally got to that appointment on Monday, the PA heard about my weekend, handed me the iPad, and then prescribed two medications when my results confirmed I was anxious and depressed. I went home and couldn't get myself to take either of them. The same tendencies that had me freaking out about my blood pressure had me struggling to put something new in my body. The doctor's appointment was helpful for a few days to believe that my heart was healthy, but it didn't have a lasting impact on my OCD and other mental health struggles.

A couple of months later, after more and more bouts in these areas, I stumbled into the office of Jonathan Schmidt, MD, attempting to find an answer. The experience I had with him was unlike anything I had seen before. He actually sat and listened to me. He knew quick answers wouldn't sustain me long term, so he sought to get to the bottom of the issues I was experiencing. As a Christian, he helped me balance faith, struggle, and therapy. I've told him this before—I feel he saved my life in the months that followed.

He has a great perspective, so I set up an interview to ask him some questions about what he's seeing in the conversation on mental health.

Can you talk through some of the science of mental illness?

The science behind why and exactly how mental illness occurs, nobody really knows. Similarly, we don't know *why* someone is awake or *why* someone is conscious. For mental illness, we do know that happier people have more serotonin in their brains. But I can't look at you and say, "Aaron, your personality is this way because of x." There's no specific gene. So everybody I meet is a blank slate. I ask them to walk me through their struggles and let's talk about it.

At this point, we just know that people who struggle with depression do better when we increase their serotonin levels. But I don't know that the problem is simply a serotonin deficiency. I think we've somehow found a medication that tweaks things and makes things better. For those with other instances of mental illness, like schizophrenia and bipolar, we've seen that they need dopamine, and that's just a different biochemical hormone. We don't fully know the why behind the effectiveness of the medicine. We just know that serotonin brings more happiness.

There's the illusion that doctors know everything or that science is so far into the future. But for mental health, we're still learning a lot. And the learnings go beyond medicine. We also know that therapy plays a role in getting healthier. We know that connection, relationships, and exercise also increase serotonin. Medicine works, and therapy works just as well. A lot of people look at that and realize that therapy takes a lot of time and taking a pill doesn't, but what's really impressive is when someone puts both together and they see an exponential increase in their serotonin and, thus, their happiness.

I recently saw an article on mental health with the tagline, "Nobody wants to live to be one hundred if they can't enjoy life." And I think that's so true. In life, we're all on a journey and have some guardrails to keep us moving along that path. For many people, but I'm not even sure that it's the majority anymore, they are weaving their way through the ups and downs on that journey, and the guardrails are helping them to keep going.

In mental illness, one of those guardrails has been decimated, and people can get stuck outside the intended path. And the thing is someone can be depressed and be outside of the guardrails and just keep pushing through. They are still showing up at home and work and masking their symptoms.

And I think there's a ton of people who are doing that. I think so many people portray happiness on the outside even though they aren't happy. They are having all the success at work and building great relationships at home. But if someone isn't healthy mentally, then they can't actually enjoy any of those things. And that's why people end up in some really dark spaces.

It's been shown that to have better physical health in your eighties, you have to have solid mental health in your fifties with good relationships. That speaks to the impact that mental health can have on your overall physical health and well-being.

So how big of an issue is this really? There seems to be a lot more talk about it now than several years ago. Is any of it blown out of proportion?

We're still so far behind where we need to be. We need to grow in our awareness of the issue. There are a lot of people who are feeling anxious or feeling depressed, and they don't have the terminology for it. Or they've felt that way for so long that they've just normalized their experience and they don't seek treatment. So awareness is a big deal. Hardly anybody comes into an appointment with me and says, "I'm depressed." Like all of us, they've only ever experienced life through their eyes, and that's all they know.

For someone who is pathologically depressed, they may not realize it until someone sits down and prompts a conversation with them about their life and how they're really doing. When I listen to people in this spot, I try to help them see that there truly is a better way. There is some help available; it's not just supposed to be this way.

A big problem is the stigmas, however. When I start talking about it with a patient and mention depression, I can tell that we're still fighting against a stigma where few people are eager to raise their hand to say they're depressed, see a psychiatrist, or be on medication. Even when it's pointed out to them how much it's holding them back or how much it's affecting their life, there is still a lot of hesitation around naming it.

As much as it's being talked about today, mental illness doesn't yet have wide-enough acceptance. There's still the thought that mental illness affects only the people who need to be institutionalized. Few people are really saying, "Oh, that's me." I think everybody struggles with their mental health to some degree. Some people are fortunate and don't struggle a lot with it; others aren't as fortunate, and it's a big part of their life.

Is society ahead of the Church in the conversation, or are both far behind where we need to be?

Well, it's like asking if you're in second to last place or if you're in last place. To me, both are lagging so far behind.

In the church, I've definitely heard sermons and podcasts where it's lightly touched on, but we certainly don't talk about it as much as we talk about other things. And if you factor in how many people in the church are dealing with it, even people who don't want to admit it, then we're not talking about it enough. But it's an uncomfortable subject, and I'm also not sure that giving a forty-minute sermon on it is the best way to do it. A lot of the progress will happen in smaller groups where people can be more vulnerable. Most people aren't going to open up in front of a large church about this.

It brings me back to the comment you mentioned—someone questioning why churches are placing broken people in leadership positions. We're all broken. We're all struggling. But for some reason, there are consequences to admitting that. That has to change. Can struggle and faith coexist? I think they absolutely have to. It's not about whether or not we will have struggles in life. It's more about enjoying the journey, which, I know, is so cliché to say.

But as an example, I own a boat, and I've heard that the best two days of boat ownership are the day you buy it and the day you sell it because boats take a lot of work. Something always seems to be breaking. And they take tons of work when you're out on the water. So you've got to enjoy the labor of it, or you're not going to like owning a boat.

That's one of the things I'm trying to teach my kids—life is a struggle. You've got to learn to enjoy it. You can't expect that you will have a smooth-sailing life, where everything goes well. That's not going to happen. We need to find happiness in day-to-day things and focus on that. I think you do that by making the world smaller.

If you think about your time with your friends, your work, your family, or your kids—if your mental health is interfering with those things, that's when you really have to take action. There's a big difference between pathological depression like that and being sad over a specific situation.

Who is the onus on to initiate this conversation?

I'm unaware of a way to make it where somebody struggling with mental health will get better if they don't participate—if they don't admit it. You can't get help without that initial step. We all crave relationships, so breaking this down with an accountability partner or someone you can walk through life with is so important. If you're married, it's essential that you can be completely vulnerable with your spouse. If you're not married, then you need someone you can trust to be able to share those things with.

I think many of us can go back to when we were kids and remember that we started to wall ourselves off at some point. Maybe we shared how we felt and got a poor response or were made fun of because of it. When that happens, regardless of how old we are, we learn not to talk about how we feel because it always leads to bad things. Someone struggling with mental health takes a leap of faith to open up, but if it's with the wrong person, it makes everything worse.

That's one of the reasons it's so tough to treat because you're asking somebody who's already struggling to be vulnerable, and they may have been burned by doing that in the past. I think the church is a wonderful place to try and foster those types of relationships. From what the church stands for, people should get a lot more acceptance, care, and understanding there.

Even in those relationships, though, at some point, if it's pathologic, all of the friendship, care, and empathy that others can provide isn't going to be enough. We may need additional support, and that's where the medical community can come in with medication and therapy to help.

I know a big priority for your practice is spending more time with each patient to understand where they're at and what treatment would be best for them. That seems critical in determining mental illness—is that the case?

Yeah, I believe direct primary care is the future of medicine and the solution to the healthcare problem because the more doctors who can offer priority, personal service, the more people who get to experience it. Right now, so much of the pressure in this conversation is being put on the patient. The person suffering has to be their own advocate, and it's on them to bring it up. That's awful.

And that's not consistent with physical illness. You don't walk in with a cold, and I sit over here as your doctor and wait for you to bring up pneumonia and tell me you have that before I address it. That would be ridiculous.

But with mental health, that's unfortunately how it works in the traditional system. If doctors cannot spend adequate time with the patient, we're counting on the person struggling to have a close friend or relative who can guide them through it and help them get to a doctor if needed.

So many doctors don't have the time to really take time with this, and you can't rush a conversation about mental health. So just like society has put up some walls, I think doctors put up some too because they don't have much time to devote to it. That's so unfortunate.

A big part of my role as a doctor is to provide hope. When you struggle with mental health, it can be easy to miss that, but we all need to have some hope on the horizon. My job is to present that and say, "Okay, here's the plan—we're going to get you better, and there are better days ahead."

One of the significant barriers for me to begin taking medicine were some of the unknowns of the medication, especially the side effects. I shared that with my good friend, Anne, and she said, "Have you thought about the side effects of living with OCD?" That was a big turning point for me to really consider medication. What are some of the stigmas around medication or the side effects we're living through without it?

That was really insightful of her to point out, and it's so true. If it's a pathological issue, it's most likely interfering with many different areas of your life. And most people don't even realize that or how bad it's affecting them because that's all they've experienced, and they believe that's how it's supposed to be.

It's hard to see at the moment, but if you can have moments of self-reflection to look back and say, "Wow, I used to feel so much different ... so much better," you can take steps toward getting better. At a certain point, not making a decision about treatment *is* making a decision. You're deciding to continue living the way you currently are, which can be as bad, if not worse, than trying medicine and failing. Every medication has side effects, but nothing has worse side effects than doing nothing at all.

I know I'm biased because of my work and the patients I see. However, the stigmas around medicine are so deep and ingrained in many parts of our society.

From your perspective, what impact are the stigmas having on the conversation? What can people do to help change those narratives?

It breaks my heart when I hear that people have heard they don't have enough faith if they struggle with their mental health. No, that's not the way any of this works. But if you've never experienced it, or if you've never had someone close to you live with it, then you may not fully understand it.

Nobody would ever say "just walk it off" if it was a broken leg because that's obviously the wrong treatment. But people always make those comments about mental health because they haven't experienced it. For someone who's really struggling with pathological mental illness, to be told to be happier, for example, does nothing and is incredibly insulting.

We all need to be more conscious of it and wisely choose our words, especially if we haven't suffered in this area. If that's the case, maybe we're lacking some perspective and need to be more aware of how we respond. We shouldn't be responding off the cuff even if we're trying to be helpful.

But we should try to be present with people because medication isn't the answer for everyone. Having a supportive person around you can have a similar effect as some medication. If people can open up to someone who can just go for a walk with them and receive their story, that may be the thing they need.

Are you seeing that a common denominator in people who struggle with mental illness is some type of isolation?

Yes, but it's difficult to know. A depressed person could have a community of people around them. Their interactions could be very social. But they may not have someone who they can be open with.

If we can differentiate a little bit between women and men, I think, men, for whatever reason, don't want to be vulnerable. I see the same story over and over and over again with men. If they had been more willing to intertwine their lives with other men around them, they wouldn't have ended up in such a dark place. And that's an excellent opportunity for the church to call that out and help foster environments and situations where both men and women can get around other people who are struggling and go through life with them.

Can you touch on that hurdle for men a little more? What's the reason for the lack of vulnerability that you see?

Maybe because I'm a man, my patient panel has unintentionally migrated more toward men over time. So I've thought a lot about this. I would say that women are suffering just as much in the areas of mental illness. I do, however, see some differences in how it's being expressed in men.

This doesn't apply to every man, but look at a typical business environment where everybody's competing against each other. Any sign of "weakness" can be used against you. So many men try to hide anything that could set them back.

Going back to that comment you've talked about, where someone asked why broken men are being put in positions of leadership, I mean, if someone believes that and thinks that if you struggle with mental health, then you won't be a good leader, the trajectory of your career is affected because of it. So we end up where we're at now with a lack of openness.

Take pilots, for example. This is constantly evolving, but there have been rules in place from the Federal Aviation Administration to ground pilots struggling with mental health. That's tough for me to understand. Rules like that enforce the stigmas and don't remove the pilot's struggle. All it does is make it so that they can't talk to anyone about it. You'd really rather have a pilot who is depressed than one who is taking antidepressants? I think many men have learned to wall themselves off from this conversation. As a result, they get so isolated. Even though they're surrounded by people, they're lonely.

What would you say to a Christian struggling with mental health right now?

Well, a lot of things go through my mind. First, I'd legitimize it. That's one of the things I can't stand—when people act like mental health struggles aren't even a real thing. I'd want them to know that what they're going through is real. I'd affirm that it's okay to struggle with this.

Then I'd encourage them to share it with someone they can trust. What I wouldn't do is just lay out the game plan to get better or tell them what they need to do. There are no one-liners that are going to change things for them. I've got to allow people to go on the journey so that they can determine if they want to seek treatment. One visit to a doctor doesn't fix this immediately—it's a process.

But if they give me the opportunity, I'd try to help them see how mental illness affects their day-to-day and encourage them that it doesn't have to be like this. We can put together a plan to help. If you're on the receiving end of someone asking for help, you've got to either commit to helping that person or connect them with other resources who can.

Ask Yourself

- How can the church be more of a safe place for people to be honest about mental illness?
- What physical side effects have you had related to your mental illness?
- Are there any tangible action steps you need to take after reading this chapter, especially pertaining to your overall health?

FINAL ENCOURAGEMENT

Vulnerability is not winning or losing; it's having the courage to show up and be seen when we have no control over the outcome. Vulnerability is not weakness; it's our greatest measure of courage.
—Dr. Brené Brown, *Rising Strong: The Reckoning. The Rumble. The Revolution.*

Say it louder for the people in the back, Brené. Vulnerability is having the courage to continue showing up. Despite the narrative we should conquer our mental struggles tomorrow, that's not what our target should be. Pray adamantly for that, yes. Believe in a God that can absolutely give us that. But then it's in his hands. And our job is just to keep showing up every day, ready to battle.

In his book *You Have What It Takes*, John Eldredge says every man asks one question throughout his life, from when he's a boy through adulthood. The question is, "Do I have what it takes?"

I don't have any proof we all ask that question, but being a man and raising three sons, I certainly think it's applicable. However, I believe men and women are searching for this answer in the battle for mental health. *Do I have what it takes to get through this? Do I have what it takes to keep showing up? Do I have what it takes to endure the pain and patiently wait for my prayers to be answered?* Maybe you've read eleven chapters of this book and are still unsure if you've got what it takes. Can I have one more attempt to convince you?

Throughout scripture, we get a front-row seat to many accounts of suffering, pain, and grief. What we *never* see in those accounts are people who had what it took to completely handle the situation on their own. Instead, we see a God who meets his people in utter wreckage and proves over and over *he has what it takes*. In any and every situation, he is truly all we need.

Some of us have been searching for an answer of "Yes! I promise you've got this. It'll be better soon!" And those answers are out there if you keep looking. But *they're not true*. Despite my best attempts and relentless effort, I haven't figured anything out on my own. And honestly, accepting my inability has been *freeing*. It's not up to me. I've tried to solve it, and I failed.

So now I just want to be found faithful. I want to keep showing up, not cower from the fight. I want to be vulnerable and courageous and inspire others to look to Jesus amid their suffering. After all, we have a God who can identify with us in every way. And he's ready to help shoulder the load.

In one message, where Spurgeon is under a substantial mental weight, he captures the beauty of our walk with Jesus so well:

> This morning, being myself more than usually compassed with infirmities, I desire to speak, as a weak and suffering preacher, of that High Priest who is full of compassion: and my longing is that any who are low in spirit, faint, despondent, and even out of the way, may take heart to approach the Lord Jesus. Let no man be afraid of him who is the embodiment of gentleness and compassion. Though conscious of your

own infirmities, you may feel free to come to him, who will not break the bruised reed, nor quench the smoking flax. I want to speak so tenderly that even the despairing may look up, and may feel a drawing towards our beloved Master who is so graciously touched with a feeling of our infirmities.[9]

Are you low in spirit, faint, despondent, out of the way, or in despair? If so, look up! See a Jesus who has walked the path you're walking and promises to lead you through it time and time again. My prayer is that you know how much he loves you today, not if you get cleaned up, not if you figure everything out, but how much he adores you *just as you are.*

Do you believe that? Do you believe you're worthy of his love regardless of your current experience? That he adores you, wants what's best for you, and would do anything for you?

Romans 5:8 (NLT) says, "But God showed his great love for us by sending Christ to die for us while we were still sinners."

You don't have to do anything to earn it. In fact, you can't. You can just keep showing up. Keep fighting. Call out the lies and refute them. God will prove himself faithful. His desires for you are even greater than anything you want for yourself. That's the love and heart of your Father.

You've heard throughout this book you don't need to do any of this alone. Many resources are available to help, some of which are listed on my website: aaronhooverwrites.com. If these aren't the right ones for you, find different ones. The resources listed are not an exhaustive attempt, and there may be better resources based on your location. Please, please, please—whatever you do, don't go at it alone.

---

[9] https://www.spurgeon.org/resource-library/sermons/the-tenderness-of-jesus/ #flipbook/

Ask Yourself

- How does it feel to know God can identify with us in every way?
- Do you believe you're worthy of the love of Jesus? If you're struggling to accept that love or understand how it could apply to you, pray and ask that he would show you how much you mean to him.
- Once you shut this book, grab your phone and reach out to someone who you can talk to. Make the choice to not go at this alone.

ABOUT THE AUTHOR

Aaron Hoover has lived with clinical anxiety, depression, and OCD for more than two decades and has seen God's faithfulness in the midst of pain. He is a pastor at Traders Point Christian Church in Indianapolis, Indiana. He has served in full-time ministry there for eight years and holds a bachelor's in religious studies and a master's in evangelism and church planting. He and his wife Megan share three world-changing sons: Wesley, Abram, and Roman.

Printed in the USA
CPSIA information can be obtained
at www.ICGtesting.com
JSHW022354270324
60039JS00001B/4